STARTING OVER
WITH GOD'S GRACE AND MERCY

Affirmations, Encouragement, and Inspiration through Bible Stories and Verses

Published by Brooks Books, Inc.

A.S. Brooks, JD

STARTING OVER WITH GOD'S GRACE AND MERCY

Published by Brooks Books, Inc.:

Brooks Books, Inc.
1775 Eye Street, NW
Washington, DC 200006

The goal of Brooks Books, Inc. is to inspire, encourage and affirm those that are seeking their footing in this world, while accepting and recognizing the challenges that persists. It is understood that with one positive touch, the world could be changed for the better!

Logo is a trademark of Brooks Books, Inc.

Library of Congress Preassigned Control Number:

ISBN: 978-1-7366508-0-6 Paperback
ISBN: 978-1-7366508-1-3 Ebook
ISBN: 978-1-7366508-4-4 Audiobook

Brooks Books, Inc. Paperback Printing: October 2021

Bible Quotation Policy:

Scriptures marked KJV are taken from the KING JAMES VERSION (KJV): KING JAMES VERSION, public domain.

Scripture quotations are from The ESV® Bible (The Holy Bible, English Standard Version®), copyright © 2001 by Crossway, a publishing ministry of Good News Publishers. Used by permission. All rights reserved.

Scripture quotations marked NLT are taken from the *Holy Bible*, New Living Translation, copyright © 1996, 2004, 2015 by Tyndale House Foundation. Used by permission of Tyndale House Publishers, Inc., Carol Stream, Illinois 60188. All rights reserved.

Scriptures marked NCV are taken from the NEW CENTURY VERSION (NCV): Scripture taken from the NEW CENTURY VERSION®. Copyright© 2005 by Thomas Nelson, Inc. Used by permission. All rights reserved.

Scriptures marked NIV are taken from the NEW INTERNATIONAL VERSION (NIV): Scripture taken from THE HOLY BIBLE, NEW INTERNATIONAL VERSION ®. Copyright© 1973, 1978, 1984, 2011 by Biblica, Inc.™.

Used by permission of Zondervan Scriptures marked NKJV are taken from the NEW KING JAMES VERSION (NKJV): Scripture taken from the NEW KING JAMES VERSION®. Copyright© 1982 by Thomas Nelson, Inc. Used by permission. All rights reserved.

Credit Line:

Cover Design by Adnan Hussain
Book Layout by Adnan Hussain
Front Photo © Can Stock Photo Inc.

Printed in the United States of America

Invitation to the Brooks Books Family!

Brooks Books, Inc. understands that your time and money are valuable! We would like to offer you insightful, encouraging as well as engaging books, music and other media.

Please go to www.BrooksBooks.org or www.BrooksReads.com and tell us your preferences or leave a comment on our blog. We want to hear from you.

By providing your email, we will enroll you in periodic giveaways, discount programs, information about events, and new releases. Look for us on Facebook, Twitter and Instagram.

Thank you for being a member of our family!

"I CAN DO ALL THINGS THROUGH CHRIST WHO STRENTHENS ME."

Philippians 4:13(NKJV)

TABLE OF CONTENTS

May Grace and Peace be Yours in Abundance!

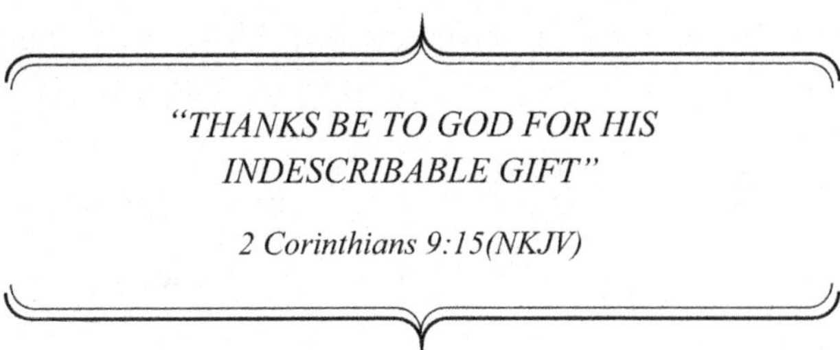

"THANKS BE TO GOD FOR HIS INDESCRIBABLE GIFT"

2 Corinthians 9:15(NKJV)

ACKNOWLEDGMENTS

How do I thank God for my life and all who have played a part in it, making it beautifully complex and filled with contradictions? Would a simple "thank you" be sufficient? My heart and soul are thankful, and I am filled with gratitude. It is my hope that this book be used to encourage others, as the word of God has encouraged me.

My mother, Maxine Smith, has been my inspiration and resource for the continued teaching and reflecting on the word of God. My father, Rupert W. Smith, desired to hear God's word, and that desire was shared. My friend and motivator, my aunt, Mae C. Johns, her wisdom and patience allowed for "possibilities" through the awareness of "what could be?" My uncle, Jerald Johns, who I refer to as "the most loved uncle," has shared his experiences and beliefs through good old-fashioned debate, making the world more interesting. His artwork and photography were provided, however, due to the cost to publish in color, I did not include them in this book. It was disappointing, but I appreciate his participation. My constant companion, spouse and friend, Kevin E. Brooks, has been a man of his word and has been consistently present in my life, which has brought stability and peace. God has so lovingly placed each of you in my life. I am blessed to have and to have had your kindness, thoughtfulness, and insightfulness.

Lastly, I am thankful that God sent his only begotten son, Jesus Christ, to die on the cross for me. He is the living sacrifice who provides salvation through faith and the Holy Spirit. His sufficiency has been proven through my trials and tribulations. The word of God which is shared through this book has inspired me.

"THERE, IF ANYONE IS IN CHRIST, HE IS A NEW CREATION; OLD THINGS HAVE PASSED AWAY; BEHOLD, ALL THINGS HAVE BECOME NEW"

2 Corinthians 5:17 (NKJV)

PROLOGUE

Starting over is hard to do, especially the older we get! And starting over is particularly difficult in this age of Covid-19! What is this thing called "starting over"? The dictionary says, "starting over" means "to make a new beginning." When the job you've had for years and rely upon has been taken from you. When the parent, spouse, or friend that you loved is sick or has died. When your business that you have invested in over the years has been forced to close. When you may not have the money to pay your mortgage or rent. When you or your loved one is suffering with an illness or disease and there is nothing you can do for them that offers hope and prayers, knowing their life is in God's hands. When you cannot hold or be held by your family and friends, knowing you must stay six feet apart. When life has been turned upside down through no fault of your own. Starting over doesn't feel good.

Despite the past, new beginnings can offer a second chance at life; an adventure worth taking to determine what new things life has to offer. But sometimes, a broken heart, fear, anger, resentment, etc., makes it difficult to see any benefits of starting anew. Who wants to let go of the past? The only thing that is known for sure. What will the future hold?

What will that future look like without the job, business or the family member, or friend? Who wants to forget who they knew, what they owned, what they valued, and what made them the way they were, the good old days?

It is good to know that a new beginning does not require that the past be forgotten. But it requires that the present and future be embraced. Perspectives must change. A new beginning is a fresh new start filled with the history and experiences as well as the pain and joy of the past, but with the wisdom and maturity that can apply to the present. Isaiah 43:18-19 (ESV) says, ***"Remember not the former things, nor consider the things of old. Behold, I am doing a new thing; now it springs forth, do you not perceive it? I will make a way in the wilderness and rivers in the desert."*** This is an important Bible verse because it lets you know that the old things have come and gone, behold the new. It also serves as a reminder of God's greatness and what he can do for you now.

The author of the following quote is unknown; however, it speaks directly to starting over.

> *"When God gives you a new beginning, it starts with an ending. Be thankful for closed doors. They often guide us to the right one."*

This quote reminds us that new beginnings help direct us to the right place, to find our purpose and to discover the joy of living. The closed doors prevent us from making the same mistake or lingering too long over something that we cannot change.

A new beginning is starting from where you are! It was said that a new beginning means to start again. However, it is also an acknowledgement that this is not the first time you changed, modified, or started on a fresh path. In the New Testament of the Bible, a Pharisee named Nicodemus, a ruler of the Jews, came to Jesus by night and said to him, ***"Rabbi, we know that you are a teacher come from God; for no one can do these signs that You do unless God is with him."*** (John 3:2)(NKJV) Jesus responded to him by saying, ***"Most assuredly, I say to you, unless one is born again, he cannot see the Kingdom of God."*** (John 3:3)(NKJV) Nicodemus was trying to figure out how he can be reborn. He pondered on the statement, trying to figure out how a man could go back into his mother's womb to be reborn. He asked Jesus, ***"How can a man be born when he is old? Can he enter a second time into his mother's womb and be born?"*** (John 3:4)(NKJV)

Nicodemus took Jesus literally. What Nicodemus misunderstood was the fact that being born again, or starting over, does not mean he had to come out of his mother's womb. It meant that he had to take actions that allowed him to be born again as a follower of Christ. Just as you have to take actions that will allow you to move from where you are to where you will find your purpose and joy. You will begin again with the skills, knowledge, and wisdom that you have already acquired. Be prepared to use them for the future and add some new ones. Remember, Nicodemus had to be reborn in spirit. Starting over requires actions that are physical, mental, and emotional!

The Apostle Paul said that although it came with tremendous effort, he had to forget what was behind him and push forward to what was ahead. He had been a persecutor of Christians, now he would lead them. In Philippians 3:13-14 (NIV), he says, "***Brothers and sisters, I do not consider myself yet to have taken hold of it. But one thing I do: Forgetting what is behind and straining toward what is ahead, I press on toward the goal to win the prize for which God has called me heavenward in Christ Jesus.***"

Just as Nicodemus could not re-enter the womb, you cannot go back in time!

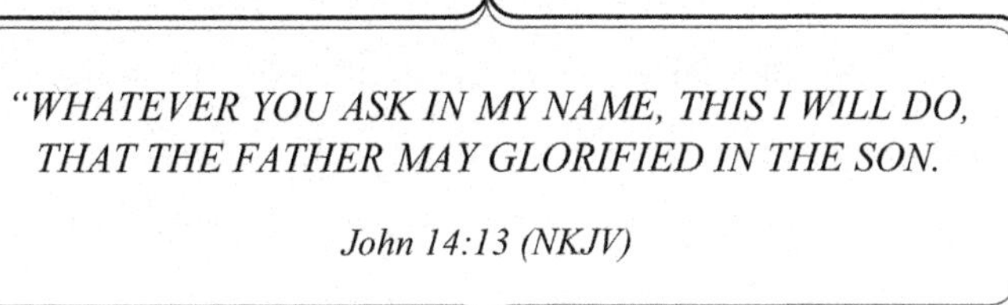

"WHATEVER YOU ASK IN MY NAME, THIS I WILL DO,
THAT THE FATHER MAY GLORIFIED IN THE SON.
John 14:13 (NKJV)

MY PRAYER FOR YOU!

It is my hope that you would be encouraged, but also find humor and wisdom that may help you through this phase of your life. The various steps that are listed contain supporting bible stories and verses that shall be a blessing to you. During my personal trials and tribulations, it put me in the position where I was encouraged to learn the Bible. It has had a tremendous impact on my life. It has led me to facilitate Bible Studies, which I enjoy tremendously. I believe it is the old stories that I knew from my childhood or stories that I never really knew that I have found interesting and uplifting.

While I am in Bible Study, I have noticed that it never fails that the group put the person we are discussing on a pedestal, not treating that person as an actual human being. For example, we recently studied Joseph, the man who married Mary, the mother of Jesus. Someone said that he was so sympathetic, and so kind and considerate to Mary when he learned she was pregnant. However, the bible said that after he found out that Mary was pregnant with Jesus, Joseph was going to quietly get out of marrying her. I had to point out that if a friend came to them and said that his girlfriend was pregnant, but he knew he did not get her pregnant because they never had sexual relations, what would the members of the group say to their friend? The answer was generally the same. Leave her, she is seeing someone behind your back! It took the angel to infiltrate Joseph's dreams to stop him from leaving her. The question that arose was whether Joseph was any different from their friend. No. He was just a human being.

The Bible consists of human beings, like you and me. We could consider it a book of sociology, history, and the formation of the church. The issues covered in the bible are vast. It is not only made up of human beings, but the bible is encouraging. If you skip to the very last book and the very last two chapters of the Bible, it tells you how it will end. The good guys win.

The Bible is not a book about winning, but it is a book about relationships. The first and foremost relationship is the one between God and man. The book of Genesis begins with God creating man. He blew life into the dirt that formed man. Life is a blessing from God. From the very beginning, in the Garden of Eden, it was the relationship with man that God desired. As you go through this difficult time, I want you to know that your life is a gift. And God wants a relationship with you.

The Old Testament of the Bible is about the Israelites starting over, again and again. God would enter a covenant with the Israelites; and they would break the covenant. God would send someone to warn them about their disobedience and they would not listen. After several hundred years, they would be punished. The punishment would be in the form of plagues, enslavement, destruction of the cities, etc. Then the Israelite people would listen to God. Only to start the cycle over again. Starting over is not new. Is God speaking to you?

The people in the Bible were real. They had their strengths and their weaknesses. Their stories may resemble yours. The way they managed their problems may be demonstrative as to how you should handle yours. The Bible provides many examples of how to resolve conflicts within the family, within the Church, and within yourself.

The most important aspect of the New Testament of the Bible is the fact that ***God so loved the world,*** including you, ***that he sent his one and only begotten Son; that whosoever believeth in him, may not perish, but may have life everlasting.*** (John 3:16)(NKJV) I want you to know that I always thought that my salvation was tied to my personal behavior. For example, how often I attended church, if I tithed, was I an usher or sung in the choir, performed a liturgy, etc., but it turns out that the grace of God saves us, not by our personal works. This is important because I want you to know that you are not being punished by God if you are in the position of starting over. Your belief in Jesus Christ is sufficient to receive God's grace. In fact, not only do you receive God's grace, but you also receive the Holy Spirit, the comforter, and the helper that transforms life.

Before you read the Steps, I would like to pray for your success. First, I pray you will be blessed with understanding. It is my prayer that you would understand that you still have a lot of life to live. You may feel as if you are tired, worn out, and simply ready to throw in the towel, but know that what you are going through is temporary. Your story has not been written.

Second, I pray you would be blessed with a vision for your life. Each person has been given the gift of life. But you have the chance to determine what will make it purposeful for you. With the proper vision, you can set your goals for the future. This might be the opportunity to envision yourself doing something completely different from before.

Third, I pray that you would have wisdom and discernment which will give you the ability to make the right decision for your life. A decision that not only helps you but would allow you to help your community too.

Fourth, I pray you will continue to grow both intellectually, psychologically, and spiritually. As you are starting over, it is my hope that you would expand in both knowledge and understanding. That your growth would allow you to see new possibilities.

Fifth, I pray that you would have strength and fortitude to withstand opposition, criticism, and disapproval. That you will forge your own path based on the desires of your heart. That you would not falter as you start again. Remember, your opinion is the only one that matters.

Sixth, I pray your experiences will not adversely affect your future. You cannot change what has already occurred, but you can move into the next phase of your life without the baggage of the past weighing you down. Your future is bright, however, the past can cause the brightness to dim, so be alert.

Seventh, I pray you will courageously accept the person who you are with all of your flaws and defects. Look around, no one is perfect! You are uniquely qualified to set the course. Many times, it is our own feeling of inferiority or failure that prevents us from moving forward. We can stand in our own way, so have courage.

Eighth, I pray you will be patient with yourself and others around you. Understand that no one lives a long life without disappointment, conflict, and failure. It takes time to formulate a plan and then to develop a strategy. Learn to be your best friend, not criticizing yourself or holding on to guilt.

Ninth, I pray you will be successful which will allow you to not only help yourself, but to help others. Success is relative. Remember, the standard for success is the one that you set for yourself.

Tenth, I pray you will experience pure joy, laughter, and happiness. Sometimes, the difficulties of life prevent us from seeing and appreciating what is positive. A good laugh can change a viewpoint. Joy can change an outlook. Happiness can affect your attitude.

Eleventh, I pray you will be loved and that you will have the capacity to love another. For love powers the desire to live, the desire to move forward, and the desire to be the best person possible. Love changes all things.

Twelfth, I pray you will put your faith in the Lord. Nothing is impossible with God.

This is my prayer for you!

"TO EVERYTHING THERE IS A SEASON,
A TIME FOR EVERY PURPOSE UNDER HEAVEN"

Ecclesiastes 3:1 (NKJV)

STEP ONE

ACKNOWLEDGE THE TIMES AND DO NOT LET FRUSTRATION SET-IN

The acceptance of your circumstance is fundamental to the possibility of change, yet frustration prevents clarity of purpose. Frustration creates stagnation. Acceptance allows for growth. It is the key to change. It sets the mark, the place where you will start over. Your history and experiences, as well as your desires and goals will merge, allowing you to plan your next step. However, if you cannot accept your circumstances, you will not be able to chart a path that is right for you. Frustration causes various negative emotions that cloud perception. For example, anger can interfere with rational thought processes. Yet anger is a product of frustration.

We are living in difficult and uncertain times. Covid-19 has upended our lives. We are not able to socialize with the ones we love, if we do, we must take precautions to keep them safe and to remain safe ourselves. Church programs, weddings, and even funerals have changed. Looking for toilet paper and paper towels was a feat at times. Many people were laid off or unemployed. Shopping malls we loved to visit are closed and now, some of our favorite shops are no longer in business. Some people who owned businesses for many years are now facing questions whether those businesses can remain operational. Businesses that we invested in for many years have closed. Some people are wondering how they are going to pay the rent, pay the mortgage or simply keep the roof over their heads. Some are even struggling with the necessities of life. For example, will their children have enough food to eat? The government officials seem to have few answers. And whether to wear a mask and keep your distance is now a question of your political party and not whether it is ethical to remain safe while keeping your neighbors safe. Children are not in school or better yet, were in school, but now home due to a Covid-19 outbreak. Family members and friends are sick. Some have died. We all have reasons to be frustrated, angry, and depressed.

Did you know the Bible states that there was a time when Jesus Christ felt sorrowful and deeply distressed? In John 13:37-38 (NIV), while speaking to several of his Disciples, he said, **"*. . . He began to be sorrowful and deeply distressed. Then He said to them,* "My soul is exceedingly sorrowful, even to death . . ."** Sorrowful is defined as sad, grieving for the loss of someone or something because of something unexpected or expected. The word "sorrowful" is not commonly used today, but depressed, distraught, discouraged, etc., is an accurate depiction of how many people describe their emotions. While speaking to Peter, Jesus felt sorrowful, even though he knew his purpose for living. Jesus told Peter that the scriptures must be fulfilled, meaning he must die on the cross, that he is the living sacrifice for our sins, that he is our Redeemer.

In Matthew 26:54 (NIV), he says, ***"How then will the Scriptures be fulfilled, which say that it must happen this way?*** "While in John 13:18 (NIV), he says, "***. . . But this is to fulfill this passage of Scripture . . .***"

Please, do not think that I am equating the trials and tribulations of the life of Jesus Christ to ours. Yet, I want you to know that we will all experience various forms of trials and tribulations that will make us feel sad, depressed, and dejected, but that we must continue to move past those feelings. We must acknowledge how we feel, however, we should not wallow in those feelings.

Don't be discouraged with the many changes in our life. We are told that it is the disappointments and failures that form character and strength. In fact, we are told that trials test faith and produce patience. We are even told to ask of God those things that reflect our desire to seek knowledge from him. If we ask, God will give wisdom liberally. James 1:2-5 (NKJV) says, ***"My brethren, count it all joy when you fall into various trials, knowing that the testing of your faith produces patience. But let patience have its perfect work, that you may be perfect and complete, lacking nothing. If any of you lacks wisdom, let him ask of God, who gives to all liberally and without reproach, and it will be given to him."***

I would like you to know and remember this truth. You are not alone, even if you feel lonely, afraid, and confused. The Apostle Paul in the first chapter of Ephesians tells us we have been blessed with every spiritual blessing in the heavenly *places* in Christ. He says that we were chosen before the foundation of the world and adopted as children. He reminds us we have been redeemed. Our sins are forgiven. It is through

God's mercy and grace that we should have faith in Jesus Christ. Ephesians 1:13 (NKJV) states, ***"In Him you also trusted, after you heard the word of truth, the gospel of your salvation; in whom also, having believed, you were sealed with the Holy Spirit of promise . . ."*** Jesus Christ told his Disciples that he must go but that he was sending a "Comforter or a Helper." John 14:26-27 (NKJV) states, **"But the Helper, the Holy Spirit, whom the Father will send in My name, He will teach you all things, and bring to your remembrance all things that I said to you. Peace, I leave with you, My peace I give to you; not as the world gives, do I give to you. Let not your heart be troubled, neither let it be afraid."**

The Bible tells us that trouble will not last! It is a temporary situation. In Ecclesiastes 3:1-8 (ESV), the author writes that there is a season for everything:

"For everything, there is a season,
and a time for every matter under heaven:

a time to be born, and a time to die;
a time to plant, and a time to pluck up what is planted;
a time to kill, and a time to heal;
a time to break down, and a time to build up;
a time to weep, and a time to laugh;
a time to mourn, and a time to dance.
a time to cast away stones, and a time to gather stones together;
a time to embrace, and a time to refrain from embracing;
a time to seek, and a time to lose;
a time to keep, and a time to cast away;
a time to tear, and a time to sew;
a time to keep silence, and a time to speak;
a time to love, and a time to hate;
a time for war, and a time for peace."

In the frustration of life, have you considered that this may be the time to rest, reflect, and restart your life? This may give you an opportunity to live an adventure, something totally different. This may be the time to incorporate a "joy" plan. However, do not be disillusioned. This is not necessarily easy. A part of reflecting on life is questioning where you are and how you got there. You must be honest because your answers will guide you to your future. Do not be afraid to question God and seek answers from him. With his direction, you will grow!

THE STORY OF THE PROPHET HABAKKUK

Are you familiar with the minor Prophet Habakkuk? He questioned God. His story is in the Old Testament of the Bible. His book comprises three chapters, an easy read. He was frustrated, angry, and confused. He surmised that those individuals that were prospering were doing so by evil means. He stated violence surrounded him. And he observed good people were being left behind and overlooked.

The book of Habakkuk opens with him questioning God. He asked how long he should cry for help because it appeared as though God wasn't even listening to him. Does that sound familiar to you? He said that there was so much violence, when would God come to the rescue. He said that he was watching wrongdoing and wickedness. The people were perverted. This led to his questions. Habakkuk 1:1-4 (MSG) states:

> ***"The problem as God gave Habakkuk to see it:***
> ***GOD, how long do I have to cry out for help***
> ***before you listen?***

How many times do I have to yell, "Help! Murder! Police!"
before you come to the rescue?
Why do you force me to look at evil,
stare trouble in the face day after day?
Anarchy and violence break out,
quarrels and fights all over the place.
Law and order fall to pieces.
Justice is a joke.
The wicked have the righteous hamstrung
and stand justice on its head."

Are you frustrated, angry, and confused, yet you are trying to do the right thing, but to no avail? Many of us can relate to the first question of Habakkuk. God answered Habakkuk's first question. God said that Habakkuk should wait and watch, that he will be amazed. He said that the nation would be overthrown. However, it will be overthrown by another nation, Babylon, but it too is wicked. God replies in Habakkuk 1:5-7 (MSG):

"Look around at the godless nations.
Look long and hard. Brace yourself for a shock.
Something's about to take place
and you're going to find it hard to believe.
I'm about to raise up Babylonians to punish you,
Babylonians, fierce and ferocious -
World-conquering Babylon,
grabbing up nations right and left,
A dreadful and terrible people,
making up its own rules as it goes."

After receiving God's answer, it led Habakkuk to ask another question. He actually began by questioning God, saying, are you not God, the Holy One, the one that existed before time? Why use this other corrupt nation to bring judgment? Habakkuk 1:12-13 (MSG) says:

> ***"God, you're from eternity, aren't you?***
> ***Holy God, we aren't going to die, are we?***
> ***God, you chose Babylonians for your judgment work?***
> ***Rock-Solid God, you gave them the job of discipline?***
> ***But you can't be serious!***
> ***You can't condone evil!***
> ***So why don't you do something about this?***
> ***Why are you silent now?***
> ***This outrage! Evil men swallow up the righteous***
> ***and you stand around and watch!"***

God did not answer Habakkuk right away. He had to wait on God for the response. Sometimes, the hardest thing to do is to wait. But waiting helps us develop patience. He says in Habakkuk 2:1 (MSG):

> ***"What's God going to say to my questions?***
> ***I'm braced for the worst.***
> ***I'll climb to the lookout tower and scan the horizon.***
> ***I'll wait to see what God says,***
> ***how he'll answer my complaint."***

When God answered Habakkuk, He told him to write his answer down. At an appointed time, Judgment will come for all men. He said that the righteous person will live because of his faithfulness, but God used several analogies to let Habakkuk know that his suffering is not in vain. Habakkuk came to accept that all things are in the hands of God and he began to understand that judgment lies with God. Knowing all men will be judged based on their character, he acknowledged God's plan. Habakkuk 2:4-8(MSG) says:

> ***"Look at that man, bloated by self-importance -***
> ***full of himself but soul-empty.***
> ***But the person in right standing before God***
> ***through loyal and steady believing***
> ***is fully alive, really alive."***
>
> ***"Note well: Money deceives.***
> ***The arrogant rich don't last.***
> ***They are more hungry for wealth***
> ***than the grave is for cadavers.***
> ***Like death, they always want more,***
> ***but the 'more' they get is dead bodies.***
> ***They are cemeteries filled with dead nations,***
> ***graveyards filled with corpses.***
> ***Don't give people like this a second thought.***
> ***Soon the whole world will be taunting them:"***
>
> ***"Who do you think you are -***
> ***getting rich by stealing and extortion?***
> ***How long do you think***
> ***you can get away with this?'***
> ***Indeed, how long before your victims wake up,***
> ***stand up and make you the victim?***
> ***You've plundered nation after nation.***
> ***Now you'll get a taste of your own medicine.***
> ***All the survivors are out to plunder you,***
> ***a payback for all your murders and massacres."***

The same issues and concerns that plagued Habakkuk also plague us, including violence, poverty, injustice, etc. When you are in the midst of trials, you cannot help but wonder if there is a God. When you are going through a tough season in your life, you may feel you are alone. That no one else could understand or know how you feel, but that is simply not true.

THE SIGNIFICANCE OF JOB

The book of Job tells the story of a man who was prosperous and faithful to God. He lost his children, his wealth, and his health because of Satan's desire to have Job curse God. His trials and tribulations are probably greater than you have experienced, yet he never cursed God, even when his wife said to do so. Even when his friends told him it was his actions that brought on his downfall.

The Book of Job opens with us being told that, "this man was blameless and upright; he feared God and shunned evil."

> ***"Job was a man who lived in Uz. He was honest inside and out, a man of his word, who was totally devoted to God and hated evil with a passion. He had seven sons and three daughters. He was also very wealthy—seven thousand head of sheep, three thousand camels, five hundred teams of oxen, five hundred donkeys, and a huge staff of servants—the most influential man in all the East!"*** Job 1: 1-3 (MSG)

There came a time when the angels came before God, along with Satan. God asked Satan where he has been and Satan said, *"**From roaming throughout the earth, going back and forth on it**."* (Job1:6)(NIV) Satan had a dialogue with God concerning the faithfulness of Job. Satan argued that if God did not protect Job and was subject to loss, he would curse God. God said to Satan, *"**Very well, then, everything he***

has is in your power, but on the man, himself do not lay a finger."(Job 1:12)(NIV) Satan began by taking Job's Oxen and Donkeys. The sheep were burned. The camels were taken. All of his children were killed. After these things, Job prayed to God, instead of cursing him as Satan had hoped:

> ***"Job got to his feet, ripped his robe,***
> ***shaved his head, then fell to the ground and worshiped:***
>
> ***Naked I came from my mother's womb,***
> ***naked I'll return to the womb of the earth.***
> ***GOD gives, GOD takes.***
> ***God's name be ever blessed.***
> ***Not once through all this did Job sin,***
> ***not once did he blame God."*** Job 1: 20–22 (MSG)

On a subsequent day, the Angels came before God, including Satan. As it concerned Job, Satan told God that Job could give up his earthly possessions, but what would happen if he himself suffered with a painful affliction, then surely Job would curse God. ***"The LORD said to Satan, "Very well, then, he is in your hands; but you must spare his life."***(Job 2:6)(NIV) Job suffered physical pain, and his wife even questioned his integrity. Job 2: 7-10 (MSG) says:

> ***"Satan left GOD and struck Job with terrible sores. Job has ulcers and scabs from head to foot. They itched and oozed so badly that he took a piece of broken pottery to scrape himself, then went and sat on a trash heap, among the ashes. His wife said, "Still holding on to your precious integrity, are you? Curse God and be done with it!" He told her, "You're talking like an empty-headed fool. We take the good days from God—why not also the***

bad days?" Not once through all this did Job sin. He said nothing against God."

Should We Accept Good from God, and Not Trouble?

Before we proceed with the story of Job, let us consider his statement, "Shall we accept good from God, and not trouble?" I have never considered asking myself this question. It feels good when everything is going great. What reasonable person does not desire to feel good all the time? But I believe there is an underlying question which is the purpose of living simply to "feel good" or is it to "do good" for one another?" Should we be seeking and maintaining a "good vibe?"

Even Job's best friends came by to support him. When they saw him, they wept; they tore their clothes, sprinkled dust on their heads, and sat with Job in silence for seven days. While sitting with his three friends, Job questioned his birth, but he did not curse God. Have you ever been so depressed that you questioned why you were born? Of course, it is human nature. Job went as far as to say that he wished he were dead, but he did not curse God. In Job 3:11-19 (MSG), he says:

"Why didn't I die at birth,
my first breath out of the womb my last?
Why were there arms to rock me,
and breasts for me to drink from?
I could be resting in peace right now,
asleep forever, feeling no pain,
In the company of kings and statesmen
in their royal ruins,
Or with princes resplendent
in their gold and silver tombs.
Why wasn't I stillborn and buried

with all the babies who never saw light,
Where the wicked no longer trouble anyone
and bone-weary people get a long-deserved rest?
Prisoners sleep undisturbed,
never again to wake up to the bark of the guards.
The small and the great are equals in that place,
and slaves are free from their masters."

BAD THINGS DO HAPPEN TO GOOD PEOPLE

Although Job's friends remained with him, they wondered, mused, speculated, considered, etc., what happened that caused these bad things to happen to Job. His friends questioned him. Surely, he must have done something wrong. They argued whether God was punishing Job for sinning against him. They were sure his circumstances were because he had done something wrong. They never considered the fact that bad things happen to good people!

There came a time when Job wanted to give up and die. He had listened to his friends and considered what they had said to him. He questioned and doubt his own actions. Job provided a lengthy reply to his friends because he didn't know what he had done wrong to God to warrant such punishment.

"Confront me with the truth and I'll shut up,
show me where I've gone off the track.
Honest words never hurt anyone,
but what's the point of all this pious bluster?
You pretend to tell me what's wrong with my life,
but treat my words of anguish as so much hot air.
Are people mere things to you?
Are friends just items of profit and loss?
"Look me in the eyes!
Do you think I'd lie to your face?
Think it over—no double-talk!

Think carefully—my integrity is on the line!
Can you detect anything false in what I say?
Don't you trust me to discern good from evil?"
Job 6: 24–30 (MSG)

Job's three friends continued to speculate about what Job had done to be punished in that manner. They were obsessed with the sins that Job could have committed, but he was at his breaking point. He said that his "Spirit is Broken." He says in Job 17:1-5 (MSG):

"My spirit is broken,
my days used up,
my grave dug and waiting.
See how these mockers close in on me?
How long do I have to put up with their insolence?
"O God, pledge your support for me.
Give it to me in writing, with your signature.
You're the only one who can do it!
These people are so useless!
You know firsthand how stupid they can be.
You wouldn't let them have the last word, would you?
Those who betray their own friends
leave a legacy of abuse to their children."

FRIENDS AND FAMILY CANNOT ALWAYS HELP YOU

Job grew weary of his friend's accusations and speculations. He says in Job 21:34 (NIV), ***"So how can you console me with your nonsense? Nothing is left of your answers but falsehood!"*** Job's friends meant well, however; the continual speculation was difficult to hear. In fact, Job called it nonsense. They were trying to determine what happened, so they do not end up in the same situation. Frustration set in. Job believed he hadn't sinned against God. He stated that what occurred was not a punishment for something that he did and that his friends' speculations were nothing more than lies.

"Bildad the Shuhite again attacked Job:

"God is sovereign, God is fearsome -
everything in the cosmos fits and works in his plan.
Can anyone count his angel armies?
Is there any place where his light doesn't shine?
How can a mere mortal presume to stand up to God?
How can an ordinary person pretend to be guiltless?
Why, even the moon has its flaws,
even the stars aren't perfect in God's eyes,
So how much less, plain men and women -
slugs and maggots by comparison!"
Job 26:1-6 (MSG)

There came a time that Job's three friends stopped speaking to him. Job 32:1(NIV)says, *"**So these three men stopped answering Job, because he was righteous in his own eyes**"* The three friends speculated, finally accusing Job of being punished by God. They determined he was guilty of something. They believed Job could not see it because of his belief in his own righteousness. Finally, the Lord spoke to Job and questioned his logic. Job 38:1-11 (MSG) states:

"And now, finally, GOD answered Job from the eye of a violent storm. He said:

"Why do you confuse the issue?
Why do you talk without knowing what you're talking about?
Pull yourself together, Job!
Up on your feet! Stand tall!
I have some questions for you,
and I want some straight answers.
Where were you when I created the earth?

Tell me, since you know so much!
Who decided on its size? Certainly, you'll know that!
Who came up with the blueprints and measurements?
How was its foundation poured,
and who set the cornerstone,
While the morning stars sang in chorus
and all the angels shouted praise?
And who took charge of the ocean
when it gushed forth like a baby from the womb?
That was me! I wrapped it in soft clouds,
and tucked it in safely at night.
Then I made a playpen for it,
a strong playpen so it couldn't run loose,
And said, 'Stay here, this is your place.
Your wild tantrums are confined to this place.'
and all the angels shouted for joy?"

After suffering with the losses of his animals, his livelihood, his children, etc., Job never cursed God. In fact, he replied to God by stating that God can do all things.

"Job answered God:

"I'm convinced: You can do anything and everything.
Nothing and no one can upset your plans.
You asked, 'Who is this muddying the water,
ignorantly confusing the issue,
second-guessing my purposes?'
I admit it. I was the one.
I babbled on about things far beyond me,
made small talk about wonders way over my head.
You told me, 'Listen, and let me do the talking.
Let me ask the questions. You give the answers.'
I admit I once lived by rumors of you;
now I have it all firsthand—from my own eyes and ears!
I'm sorry—forgive me. I'll never do that again, I promise!
I'll never again live on crusts of hearsay, crumbs of rumor."
Job 42:1-6 (MSG)

After Job had prayed for his friends, the LORD restored his fortunes and gave him twice as much as he had before.

CHANGE YOUR OUTLOOK, THERE'S BEAUTY IN YOUR LIFE

I want you to know that you must purposely look for the beauty and blessings of your life if you are going to move forward. For example, if you are reading this book, then you have eyes to see and a mind to understand. You woke up this morning; it is the beginning of a new day, a new life. More than likely, you have someone in your life, whether it is a friend, acquaintance, sister, brother, aunt, uncle, mother, father, classmate, colleague, etc. It is easy to look at the things that you do not have, but first consider those things that you have. This will open the door to different possibilities.

"TRUST IN THE LORD WILL ALL YOUR HEART, AND LEAN NOT ON YOUR OWN UNDERSTANDING"

Proverbs 3:5 (NKJV)

STEP TWO

DO NOT LET YOUR PAST DESTROY YOUR FUTURE

There is something about what happened yesterday that causes people to hold on to it, making it bigger and better. It could be the fact that your family felt complete. Now you may be dealing with the loss of a loved one, a business, a job, or simply your innocence. Do we hold on to the past because we know the outcome, the consequences for our actions? Or were we different; invincible, strong, beautiful, etc. There are so many reasons to hold on to it, but the past was yesterday, it is over, we cannot take it with us. But we can take the knowledge, the skills, the creativity, the experience, the relationships, and the belief in a better tomorrow. There is power in tomorrow, but we cannot let the past destroy it.

THE STORY OF NAOMI

I would like to tell you about a story that at first glance appears to be of loss and weariness. But it is actually a story of hope and moving forward even when you think the end is near. In the book of Ruth. We are told about the story of Naomi. We are told that she has a husband, Elimelech, and they have two sons. Their homeland was besieged with a famine. There was little water and food. They decided to move to a foreign land, Moab, until the drought was over. To Naomi's dismay, Elimelech died, leaving her heartbroken. Later, her two sons married Moab women, Orpah and Ruth. But soon, her two sons died, leaving only their wives. Not only was Naomi depressed and in mourning, but she felt God was against her. She wanted to be left alone. She told her daughters-in-law to go back to their families. She had no other sons to offer them. Orpah did as she stated, but Ruth pleaded with her and demanded to stay. Naomi was ready to give up. She remembered the joys of her life with her husband and children. She treasured her homeland. Can you imagine how Naomi must have felt about losing her home, her husband, and her two sons? We can get a glimpse of how she feels when she returns home to Bethlehem and her neighbors ask, ***"Is this Naomi?"*** In the book of Ruth 1:20-21(NKJV), Naomi responds, ***"Do not call me Naomi; call me Mara, for the Almighty has dealt very bitterly with me. I went out full, and the LORD has brought me home again empty. Why do you call me Naomi, since the LORD has testified against me, and the Almighty has afflicted me?"***

Her past could have stood in the way of her future, but survival was a necessity. Not only did Naomi have to be concerned about her future, but she had to be concerned about Ruth. Sometimes, the love of someone else helps us to get back on track. In order to find food, Ruth would go out into the fields to harvest barley. On one such occasion, Ruth came in contact with a relative of Naomi's husband, Boaz. We are told that he is ***"a man of great wealth."*** Ruth 2:1 (NKJV) Ruth catches the eye of Boaz. He puts her under his wing. He makes sure she is protected from the other men and that she has food and drink as needed.

Naomi concerned about the security of Ruth, says to her, ***"My daughter, shall I not seek security for you, that it may be well with you?"*** She came up with a plan that would allow Ruth to get close to Boaz. Naomi told Ruth, ***" Now Boaz, whose young women you were with, is he not our relative? In fact, he is winnowing barley tonight at the threshing floor. Therefore, wash yourself and anoint yourself. Put on your best garment and go down to the threshing floor; but do not make yourself known to the man until he has finished eating and drinking."*** Ruth 3:1-3 (NKJV) Ruth assured Naomi that she would follow her instructions.

Boaz laid down and went to sleep after he ate and drank. Seeing him asleep, Ruth removed his shoes and laid at his feet. When he woke and found her, he said, ***"Blessed are you of the LORD, my daughter! For you have shown more kindness at the end than at the beginning, in that you did not go after young men, whether poor or rich. And now, my daughter, do not fear. I will do for you all that you request, for all the people of my town know that you are a virtuous woman."*** Ruth 3:10-11 (NKJV) Boaz promised to contact a relative that was closer than him to marry her. If he refused to do so, Boaz, himself, would perform the duty and marry her. He also gave her six bushels of barley for Naomi. Later, Boaz met with the relative in front of the elders and other people. He asked the relative to redeem the property sold by Naomi, he agreed. Then Boaz mentioned he must take Ruth as his wife. But the relative could not agree to do it because of his own inheritance.

Therefore, Boaz agreed to redeem the property sold by Naomi and marry Ruth. They were blessed with a son, Obed. "***Then the women said to Naomi, "Blessed be the LORD, who has not left you this day without a close relative; and may his name be famous in Israel! And may he be to you a restorer of life and a nourisher of your old age; for your daughter-in-law, who loves you, who is better to you than seven sons, has borne him." Then Naomi took the child and laid him on her bosom, and became a nurse to him. Also, the neighbor women gave him a name, saying, "There is a son born to Naomi." And they called his name Obed. He is the father of Jesse, the father of David."*** Ruth 4:14-17 (NKJV)

Naomi said that she went out full, and the Lord had brought her home empty again. That is a feeling that many of us can relate to, especially after a loss. The word "full" can mean so many things. But for Naomi, it meant that her past was full of love, family, riches, security, etc. Her present circumstance was empty of that fulness. No home, no husband and no children. Just a daughter-in-law. It turned out that were daughter-in-law loved her more than seven sons! In order for Naomi to discover this blessing, she had to survive her past.

DEADLY COMBINATION OF GUILT, REGRET AND FEAR

My Father would tell me not to die with regrets and guilt. I don't think I understand the nuance of what he was saying to me. But as I have gotten older, I realize that the guilt of taking or not taking an action can have consequences that cause sleepless nights. The regret of taking actions that may have been harmful to someone else, even yourself, can be humbling. And both guilt and regret create fear.

Do you remember the story of Jacob, whose name they later changed to Israel? He was the father of the twelve tribes of Israel. But he was born a twin and his brother was Easu. Although they were twins, Easu was the firstborn. Their parents had favorites. Genesis 25:27-28 (NKJV) states, ***"So the boys grew. And Esau was a skillful hunter, a man of the field; but Jacob was a mild man, dwelling in tents. And Isaac loved Esau because he ate of his game, but Rebekah loved Jacob."***

As is the custom, the Father would bless the eldest son. As Isaac grew old and unable to see, he told his son Easu to get him some food and bring it to him. He was going to bless him when he returned. Rebekah, hearing the conversation, called Jacob what occurred. She came up with a plan to trick Isaac into giving the blessing to Jacob instead of Esau. Knowing he was wrong, he took the food that his mother cook and draped his body with his brother's garments. ***"So he went to his father and said, "My father." And he said, "Here I am. Who are you, my son?" Jacob said to his father, "I am Esau your firstborn; I have done just as you told me; please arise, sit and eat of my game, that your soul may bless me."*** Genesis 27:18-19 (NKJV)

When Esau came into his father's tent with the food and expecting a blessing, he was told by Isaac that his brother deceived him and received his blessing. Esau was distraught and, in that moment, he sought vengeance. ***"So Esau hated Jacob because of the blessing with which his father blessed him, and Esau said in his heart, "The days of mourning for my father are at hand; then I will kill my brother Jacob."*** Genesis 27:41 (NKJV)

Their mother, Rebekah, hearing of the threat, sent Jacob to her brother, Laban. He stays with Laban for over twenty years. For the first seven years he works for his love, Rachel, however, he was tricked into marrying Leah, the oldest daughter. For the next seven years, he works to gain Rachel's hand in marriage. For the next six years, he works for livestock and cattle. He leaves Laban and travels home.

As his past was almost forgotten, he was told of his brother, Esau, who wanted to see him. Esau was traveling with an entourage of four hundred men. ***"So Jacob was greatly afraid and distressed; and he divided the people that were with him, and the flocks and herds and camels, into two companies. And he said, "If Esau comes to the one company and attacks it, then the other company which is left will escape."*** Genesis 32:7-8 (NKJV) It was Jacob's own guilt that led him to believe that his brother, Esau, was still angry with him after twenty years.

It is said that Jacob was so afraid that he fought with God. "***Then Jacob was left alone; and a Man wrestled with him until the breaking of day. Now when He saw that He did not prevail against him, He touched the socket of his hip; and the socket of Jacob's hip was out of joint as He wrestled with him. And He said, "Let Me go, for the day breaks." But he said, "I will not let You go unless You bless me!" So He said to him, "What is your name?" He said, "Jacob." And He said, "Your name***

shall no longer be called Jacob, but Israel; for you have struggled with God and with men, and have prevailed." Genesis 32:24-28 (NKJV)

When Esau came to Jacob, he was delighted to see his brother. He gave him a long hug and kissed him on the neck. He even refused the cattle and other goods that Jacob was giving to him, but he later lamented after Jacob was persuasive. He had forgiven his brother. He had let the past go! It was Jacob who was guilty and could not move forward after deceiving his father and stealing the blessing from his brother. He had regrets that prevented him from anticipating a different outcome.

STRANGE TEXT

I received a strange text from one of my old clients. He asked me to call him as soon as possible. The text itself was not strange because he asked me to call him, but due to the tone. When I called him, he told me that one of my clients, his dear friend, had died. I inquired as to the cause of her death. He said that she drank herself to death. She was an alcoholic. In all actuality, she did not drink herself to death, but the alcohol caused her to be involved in a serious automobile accident that killed her.

Her story was simple. She refused to let go of the past. It defined her. I shared with her my own experiences, thinking that she would see there was a future for her. She did not believe it. Several years ago, her home had been foreclosed upon. She was forced to move out of the premises, putting part of her life in storage. She believed the bank committed fraud, which caused their actions to be illegal. I remembered speaking to her because of the advice that I gave her, the advice that I could not take myself. I told her to let go of the past because it was standing in the way of her future.

She started an accounting practice. She had several people working for her. It was my belief that she could put herself in the position of buying a new home without the depreciation from the recession from 2008 to 2009 that was still affecting the real estate market. Let me explain to you what I mean. Many people fell behind on their mortgage. They sought help from their mortgage company by way of a modification which changed the terms, allowing them to make regular monthly payments. In the last few years, many of the modifications contained provisions placing large balances as a separate debt in the back of the loan. It would not be paid through monthly payments. It would be in the form of a balloon payment that would occur after they paid the new modified principal balance off. For example, the house may have been valued at $425,000, but they may owe $575,000. The modified principal balance may have been $425,000 and the remaining balance of $150,000. This amount would be held in an account that would be paid off at the end of the term, generally thirty years. On the other hand, my client could buy a new home at the current market rates with no hidden arrears. She could take part in equity appreciation. It could have been her opportunity to start over, but she could not see it.

I was reading an article written by Leon F. Seltzer, PhD, which was published in Psychology Today called, "Don't Let Your Past Control Your Future." A statement that he made in that article dumbfounded me because it applied to both my client and myself. He stated, "What haunts most of us are the various mistakes we made in the past. Mistakes that left us feeling embarrassed, humiliated, degraded, or ashamed. And the worst part of all our missteps is that because they may have represented defining moments in our lives, we may actually define ourselves on their basis. These mistakes were driven by impulse, or reflective of what made sense to us back then. But many of the negative decisions about ourselves and the world they prompted us to adopt were, given our age and maturity, significantly over-generalized. Still, however indirectly, they've been a major influence in determining the present quality of our lives." I have found Dr. Seltzer's statements to be true. It is the mistakes, or the guilt associated with the past, that prevent many of us from moving forward.

Since I have been facilitating Bible studies on Thursdays, I have been reading and studying the Bible for practical applications versus the theory or concepts of Christianity. Its teachings are hitting home. The Bible writes about letting go of the past and starting anew. For example, in Isaiah 43:18-19 (NKJV) it says:

> ***"Do not remember the former things,***
> ***Nor consider the things of old.***
> ***Behold, I will do a new thing,***
> ***Now it shall spring forth;***
> ***Shall you not know it?***
> ***I will even make a road in the wilderness***
> ***And rivers in the desert."***

What do you think about the above verse, "Behold, I will do a 'NEW' thing"? Does it bring you hope? I want you to know that it has changed my life because I have been holding on to the old things for way too long, and I have paid for it with my health and financial circumstances. We, you and me, need to move forward together. Our memories should remind us of the adventures of our life; the ups and downs, the joy and sadness, the laughter and the crying, the people that we loved and lost, etc. We need to be thankful for our past while looking forward to our future. In fact, Proverbs 4:25-26 (NKJV) tells us to look straight ahead:

"Let your eyes look straight ahead,
And your eyelids look right before you.
Ponder the path of your feet,
And let all your ways be established."

Why do you think it is necessary to say, "Let your eyes look straight ahead"? The Apostle Paul wrote a letter to the church of Philippi. He stated he did not want his past to hinder the growth of the church, the churches' future. If you remember, he persecuted Christians with vigor and certitude. He said to forget those things that are behind, but reach forward to those things that are ahead:

> ***"Not that I have already attained, or am already perfected; but I press on, that I may lay hold of that for which Christ Jesus has also laid hold of me. Brethren, I do not count myself to have apprehended; but one thing I do, forgetting those things which are behind and reaching forward to those things which are ahead, I press toward the goal for the prize of the upward call of God in Christ Jesus. Therefore, let us, as many as are mature, have this mind; and if in anything you think otherwise, God will reveal even this to you. Nevertheless, to the degree that we have already attained, let us walk by the same rule, let us be of the same mind."***
> Philippians 3: 12–16 (NKJV)

The reason I am telling you about Apostle Paul and his letter to the Philippians is that you know you must be flexible in this life and willing to change and grow. Apostle Paul had a goal. He wanted to spread the "Good News" by establishing Churches. He could not allow his past to prevent this goal. He had to rely upon God, Jesus Christ, and the Holy Spirit.

> ***"Trust in the LORD with all your heart,***
> ***And lean not on your own understanding;***
> ***In all your ways acknowledge Him,***
> ***And He shall direct your paths."***
> Proverbs 3:5-6 (NKJV)

This Proverb speaks volumes. An article called, "Your Past Does Not Define You or Your Future," which I found on the website, Skilledatlife.com, ended with a wonderful statement that I want to share with you. It says, "Your past, no matter how bad it was, does not define your future. The choices and actions you make *today* will ultimately define who you will eventually become. Make the decision to learn from your past and apply it in the present, so that you can live the life that you were meant to live."

You deserve a future that is thought-provoking, adventuresome, and satisfying!

"I WILL PRAISE YOU, FOR I AM FEARFULLY AND WONDERFULLY MADE; MARVELOUS ARE YOUR WORKS, AND THAT MY SOUL KNOWS VERY WELL"

Psalm 139:14 (NKJV)

STEP THREE

LOVE YOURSELF OPENLY, FREELY, AND JOYFULLY

The power of love is said to be one of the most significant forces in the universe; while the acceptance of oneself enables you to love all of your strengths and weaknesses, for those characteristics make you unique. Loving yourself does not mean standing on a pedestal hollering at the top of your lungs that you are so special, so unique, that you are better than your neighbors, friends, family, strangers, and foes. It means that you recognize and approve of that which makes you, you.

We are told to love others as much as ourselves. Hence, it is assumed that we love ourselves with the understanding that our life is a blessing, a gift that we will only get once. In Matthew 22:36-40 (NKJV), Jesus Christ was asked the following, ***"Teacher, which is the great commandment in the Law?" And he said to him,*** **"You shall love the Lord your God with all your heart and with all your soul and with all your mind. This is the great and first commandment. And a second is**

like it: You shall love your neighbor as yourself. On these two commandments, the Law and the Prophets depend."

Yet, we have become our own worst critic. For example, how many times have you looked in the mirror and called yourself fat? How many times you have tried to cover up the gray hair because you felt you looked old? How many times have you tried on something that just did not fit, only to leave the store totally deflated due to your physical size? You are worth celebrating even if you are old, fat, gray, etc., because you are "you" and there is no other person like you.

THE DISCIPLE THAT JESUS LOVED

John, a disciple of Jesus Christ, was known as "the disciple that Jesus loved." It is believed that he wrote the book of John or the Gospel of John. At the Last Supper, after Jesus stated he would be betrayed, Peter reached out to John to find out who would betray Jesus. In John 13:23-24 (NKJV), he says, ***"One of his disciples, whom Jesus loved, was reclining at table at Jesus' side, so Simon Peter motioned to him to ask Jesus of whom he was speaking."***

If we were to identify ourselves as "the daughter that was loved by my mother or the son that was loved by my father," others would believe that the statement itself is a sign of our own arrogance or self-importance. Especially if their mother had several daughters or their father had other sons. But in the bible, it demonstrates the fact Jesus loved him. It does not say that the others were not loved. In some ways, the identity reflects John's humility because he could only be defined through his relationship with Jesus and the various actions that he took on behalf of Jesus throughout the gospel:

- John was one of the twelve who was with Jesus when He washed the disciples' feet and identified the one who would betray Him.
- John witnessed Jesus Christ's death on the cross and was afterward entrusted with the care of Jesus' mother.
- John was the first to see the empty tomb after Christ's resurrection.
- John was frequently paired with Peter.
- The book of Acts and the other gospels tell us that Peter and John often worked together as part of Jesus' inner circle.

This is important when we discuss our own identity. When we are confronted with the questions; what our strengths are or what are the qualities and/or characteristics that make us unique, we have a hard time answering. Many of us have received the message that if we should acknowledge those skills or talents that make us special, that we would become boastful, overly confident, maybe even arrogant. However, that is a mistake. It makes us suppress who we are. We must embrace all of our characteristics with humility and grace, not denying those gifts that make us strong or weak. The Bible says that we should be humble, proceed with humility. Proverbs 11:2 (NKJV) states, ***"When pride comes, then comes disgrace, but with the humble is wisdom."***

IDENTITY THROUGH CHRIST

As Christians, our identity is enhanced, modified, and superior. We are given spiritual gifts. First, Jesus Christ died on the cross as a living sacrifice, redeeming and forgiving us of our sins. Ephesians 1:7-10 (NIV) states, ***"In him we have redemption through his blood, the forgiveness of our trespasses, according to the riches of his grace, which he lavished upon us, in all wisdom and insight making known to us the mystery of his will, according to his purpose, which he set forth in Christ as a plan for the fullness of time, to unite all things in him, things in heaven and things on earth."*** Second, we are adopted in the body of Christ. Ephesians 1:5-6 (NIV) says, ***"In love he predestined us for adoption to himself as sons through Jesus Christ, according to the purpose of his will, to the praise of his glorious grace, with which he has blessed us in the Beloved."*** Third, we received the promise of the Holy Spirit. Ephesians 1:13-14 (NIV) states, ***"In him you also, when you heard the word of truth, the gospel of your salvation, and believed in him, were sealed with the promised Holy Spirit, who is the guarantee of our inheritance until we gain possession of it, to the praise of his glory." And*** fourth, we receive an inheritance that is filled with glory. Ephesians 1:11-12 (NIV) says, ***"In him we have obtained an inheritance, having been predestined according to the purpose of him who works all things according to the counsel of his will, so that we who were the first to hope in Christ might be to the praise of his glory."*** The world values us differently.

AS SEEN ON TV

We are in the age of social media: Facebook, Twitter, YouTube, etc. It creates its own special and unique problems. Both friends and enemies can comment and/or criticize you. Our identity and self-love can be questioned. Everything is scrutinized. What we say, why we say it, how we say it, what we look like saying it, the picture that is posted is all reviewed.

Not only do you have to worry about what people might say, but you have to worry about how many friends are following you. The more friends you may have, the more popular you become. If you only have ten friends, are you less valuable to our society? Our society has created a mechanism that requires that we are "on and connected" all the time. It is not only exhausting, but it also makes us compare ourselves to the next person. These constant comparisons make us question who we are, what we look like, and what we are doing with our lives. Turn social media off, if only for a few days, and see if you feel any better! We are growing angrier, frustrated, overwhelmed, anxiety filled, etc. Not only is it affecting you, but it is affecting the kids too.

LOVE YOURSELF

Loving yourself; openly, freely, and joyfully simply means accepting the person who you are! If you are terrible at math, so what! If you have added a few pounds, so what! If your arthritis is acting up and you are walking with a limp, so what! If you cannot hold a note, but love to sing, sing! If you are a terrible comic, but love to tell a good joke, tell it. Don't be discouraged if someone does not appreciate your effort. You must do some things for you!

King David said that he will praise God because he is "fearfully and wonderfully made." Psalms 139: 13 - 16 (NKJV) says:

"For You formed my inward parts;
You covered me in my mother's womb.
I will praise You, for I am fearfully and wonderfully made;
Marvelous are Your works,
And that my soul knows very well.
My frame was not hidden from you,
When I was made in secret,
And skillfully wrought in the lowest parts of the earth.
Your eyes saw my substance, being yet unformed.
And in Your book they all were written,
The days fashioned for me,
When as yet there were none of them."

The Apostle Paul, in his first letter to the Corinthians, wrote in depth about love, God's love, God's love for the Church. He also broke down various characteristics of Love, including the fact that love never fails. He even said that Love is greater than Faith and Hope:1 Corinthians 13:1-7(NLT):

"If I could speak all the languages of earth and of angels, but didn't love others, I would only be a noisy gong or a clanging cymbal. If I had the gift of prophecy, and if I understood all of God's secret plans and possessed all knowledge, and if I had such faith that I could move mountains, but didn't love others, I would be nothing. If I gave everything I have to the poor and even sacrificed my body, I could boast about it; but if I didn't love others, I would have gained nothing.

Love is patient and kind. Love is not jealous or boastful or proud or rude. It does not demand its own way. It is not irritable, and it keeps no record of being wronged. It does not rejoice about injustice but rejoices whenever the truth wins out. Love never gives up, never loses faith, is always hopeful, and endures through every circumstance."

Apostle Paul in the book of Ephesians tells his followers to be imitators of God and walk in Love. He reminds them that God gave his Son as a Living Sacrifice for us! Ephesians 5: 1-2 (NKJV) says, ***"therefore be imitators of God as dear children. And walk in love, as Christ also has loved us and given Himself for us, an offering and a sacrifice to God for a sweet-smelling aroma."***

We must love ourselves!

"FOR ALL HAVE SINNED
AND FALL SHORT OF THE GLORY OF GOD"

Romans 3:23 (NKJV)

STEP FOUR

FORGIVE YOURSELF
LIVE A GUILT FREE LIFE

Forgiveness is the act of pardoning an offender, and that includes pardoning yourself. When the Greeks translated the Bible, they took the word that means "forgiveness" and translated to "let go." For example, if a person was due money from an individual and they decided not to collect the debt or demand payment, they were forgiving the debt or letting it go. In Matthew 6:14-15 (NKJV), Jesus Christ taught the concept of forgiveness. He said, ***"For if you forgive men their trespasses, your heavenly Father will also forgive you. But if you do not forgive men their trespasses, neither will your Father forgive your trespasses."*** We forgive others when we let go of resentment and give up any claim to be compensated for the hurt or loss we have suffered. The same is true when you forgive yourself. Forgiveness requires letting go of guilt, blame, disappointment, hurt, etc. The Bible teaches that unselfish love is the basis for true forgiveness since love does not keep account of injury.

Jesus Christ died for you, redeeming you from sin, so long as you have chosen him. He has died for your sins and that nullifies your guilt and blame. He has forgiven you. Therefore, forgive yourself. Ephesians 4:31-32 (NIV) states, ***"Get rid of all bitterness, rage and anger, brawling and slander, along with every form of malice. Be kind and compassionate to one another, forgiving each other, just as in Christ God forgave you."***

Do you remember the Parable of the Unforgiving Servant found in Matthew 18:21-35 (NKJV)? Peter asked Jesus, ***"Lord, how often shall my brother sin against me, and I forgive him? Up to seven times?"*** Jesus responded to Peter, saying the following, ***"I do not say to you, up to seven times, but up to seventy times seven.*** Jesus continued answering by stating a parable for his followers. He said, ***"Therefore, the kingdom of heaven is like a certain king who wanted to settle accounts with his servants. And when he had begun to settle accounts, one was brought to him who owed him ten thousand talents. But as he was not able to pay, his master commanded that he be sold, with his wife and children and all that he had, and that payment be made. The servant therefore fell down before him, saying, 'Master, have patience with me, and I will pay you all.' Then the master of that servant was moved with compassion, released him, and forgave him the debt."***

"But that servant went out and found one of his fellow servants who owed him a hundred denarii; and he laid hands on him and took him by the throat, saying, 'Pay me what you owe!' So, his fellow servant fell down at his feet and begged him, saying, 'Have patience with me, and I will pay you all.' And he would not but went and threw him

into prison till he should pay the debt. So, when his fellow servants saw what they had done, they were very grieved, and came and told their master all that had been done. Then his master, after he had called him, said to him, 'You wicked servant! I forgave you all that debt because you begged me. Should you not also have had compassion on your fellow servant, just as I had pity on you?' And his master was angry and delivered him to the torturers until he should pay all that was due to him. "So, my heavenly Father also will do to you if each of you, from his heart, does not forgive his brother his trespasses."

This parable lets you know that Jesus Christ values forgiveness. It is argued that a person who cannot forgive themselves, cannot forgive others. How can you know and love yourself truly, yet fail to forgive yourself for mistakes or wrong decisions that occurred? Yet argue that you are able to love a stranger or forgive them their trespasses when you may not know or even like them as a person? Is that possible? Let go of guilt and blame, forgive yourself.

Forgiveness has other benefits as well. On November 4, 2018, there was an article published in the newsletter for Mayo Clinic called, "Forgiveness: Letting go of grudges and bitterness." It lists the health benefits of forgiveness:

- Healthier relationships
- Improved mental health
- Less anxiety, stress, and hostility
- Lower blood pressure
- Fewer symptoms of depression
- A stronger immune system

- Improved heart health
- Improved self-esteem

Remember, Romans 3:23(NKJV) says, ***"For all have sinned and fall short of the glory of God."***

FAILURE

It is easy to become frustrated and disappointed when you believe you have done your best, only to fail. In some ways, there is nothing more demoralizing than failure because it denotes that the actions taken were insufficient. This can cause a rational person to be afraid to change, modify or take a risk due to the fear of failure. They can demonstrate this fear through various actions or no action at all, such as procrastinating, second guessing oneself, or seeking direction from someone else. The dictionary defines failure as the lack of success. But for many people, it is much more than just lacking success. It is being knocked down. Starting over after feeling defeated can be a daunting task, but faith and hope are necessary to overcome fear.

James 1:2-5 (NIV) states, *"**Consider it pure joy, my brothers and sisters, whenever you face trials of many kinds, because you know that the testing of your faith produces perseverance. Let perseverance finish its work so that you may be mature and complete, not lacking anything. If any of you lacks wisdom, you should ask God, who gives generously to all without finding fault, and it will be given to you.**"*

The author of the book of James made two arguments pertaining to trials and tribulations. The first is that trials and tribulations are provisional, it is only temporary. The second is that the trials and tribulations are purifying, for a purpose greater than what is at hand. In other words, they are lessons that are meant to produce perseverance. James 1:12 (NIV) states, ***"Blessed is the one who perseveres under trial because, having stood the test, that person will receive the crown of life that the Lord has promised to those who love him."***

We should get a tremendous amount of joy from the book of James because he is not only saying that trials and tribulations are temporary and for a greater good, but that if you continue with your walk, persevere, you will receive the crown of life. This does not mean that you will not fail in life; it means that even if you fail, continue to move forward, and continue to try, for a blessing awaits you.

As a bankruptcy attorney, I counseled people who were in debt. There was a common thread among them. They felt they caused their particular dilemma, that they were to blame, but they could not quite put their hands on when their downfall occurred at the precise moment. What decision did they make that caused them to be where they were? If it is a man, who is a husband and has kids, this dilemma usually is particularly disheartening because he is supposed to take care of his family. He is the head of the house. He failed. If it is a woman who could buy her own home and take care of her family, she usually would doubt who she is and what value she's brought to her family. I do not know how many times I have said, "The only way you would have known what the future held is if you had a crystal ball" or, "if only you had a money tree in your backyard."

I would say that 99.9% of the people I counseled were good, hardworking people, one or two generations away from poverty. They wanted to do the right thing. They wanted to go to work, earn a living, take care of themselves as well as their families, keep a roof over their head, etc. They did not want to depend on others. Most lost their jobs because of layoffs or downsizing. Some people were involved in accidents or suffered from serious illness. Usually, their circumstances were due to no fault of their own.

So, they spoke to me, in the convenience of my office, knowing their conversation will not only be private but confidential. They cried. A heartfelt cry. They blamed themselves. How do you let go of the hurt, how do you forgive yourself for not having a crystal ball or a money tree to rely upon when you are in financial turmoil? How do you forgive yourself for not knowing the right words or the right road to take to safety? How do you forgive yourself for not knowing a cure, for not being able to save your loved one? Each situation may be different, but in the end, it requires the same act, the act of forgiveness.

FEAR

At the root of most people's anxiety is fear, and it is legitimate. There are many causes of fear including (a) fear of the unknown, uncertainty and doubt, (b) not having control to change or steer their circumstances, (c) the belief that they may suffer either physical, emotional, or psychological pain, (d) environment dangers, such as wildfires, flooding, tornadoes, etc., (e) situations or objects, such as flying, snakes, spiders, etc., the list could go on and on. Fear is defined as a distressing emotion aroused by impending danger.

Fear can cripple and can push the most composed person into a state of utter discomfort and uncertainty, but the Bible reminds us we should not fear, for fear does not come from God. Fear prevents you from having a peace of mind, keeping you and your thoughts in chaos. Even though we are not promised perfection in this life, we should find comfort in knowing that we are promised salvation, which will give us life everlasting with God.

Did you know that the term "fear not" is stated in the Bible 365 times, which ironically, is the same amount of days in a year? Some recognizable Scripture verses containing 'fear not' include Isaiah 41:10 (NKJV), ***"Fear not, for I am with you; Be not dismayed, for I am your God. I will strengthen you, Yes, I will help you, I will uphold you with My righteous right hand." Another*** verse that is popular is Joshua 1:9 (NKJV), which states, ***"Have I not commanded you? Be strong and of good courage; do not be afraid, nor be dismayed, for the Lord your God is with you wherever you go."*** And 2 Timothy 1:7 (NKJV) which says, ***"For God has not given us a spirit of fear, but of power and of love and of a sound mind."***

But the scripture that is most often quoted is ***"Trust in the LORD with all your heart, and do not lean on your own understanding. In all your ways acknowledge him, and he will make straight your paths. Be not wise in your own eyes; fear the LORD and***

turn away from evil. It will be healing to your flesh and refreshment to your bones." Proverbs 3:5-8 (NKJV)

I would like to discuss a story found in 2nd Chronicles, the 20th chapter. I was able to find comfort and relief because it shows the steps taken by a king who was terrorized by fear. Anyone can take the steps he took to help alleviate their fear. The King of Judah, King Jehoshaphat, was under siege by other rulers. He turned to the Lord for help. It begins by stating the following:

"Then some came and told Jehoshaphat, saying, "A great multitude is coming against you from beyond the sea, from Syria; and they are in Hazazon Tamar" (which is En Gedi). And Jehoshaphat feared, and set himself to seek the LORD, and proclaimed a fast throughout all Judah. So, Judah gathered together to ask help from the LORD; and from all the cities of Judah they came to seek the LORD (2nd Chronicles 20:2-4) (NKJV)

Step One: What is important to note here is that Jehoshaphat sought the Lord

Step Two: Jehoshaphat took action by proclaiming a fast throughout Judah

**Step Three: Jehoshaphat joined forces with others.

Continuing, "***Then Jehoshaphat stood in the assembly of Judah and Jerusalem, in the house of the LORD, before the new court, and said: "O LORD God of our fathers, are You not God in heaven, and do***

You not rule over all the kingdoms of the nations, and in Your hand is there not power and might, so that no one is able to withstand you? Are You not our God, who drove out the inhabitants of this land before Your people Israel, and gave it to the descendants of Abraham Your friend forever? And they dwell in it and have built You a sanctuary in it for Your name, saying, 'If disaster comes upon us—sword, judgment, pestilence, or famine—we will stand before this temple and in Your presence (for Your name is in this temple), and cry out to You in our affliction, and You will hear and save." 2nd Chronicles 20:5-9) (NKJV)

Step Four: Jehoshaphat prayed to the Lord. Within that prayer, he questioned God by asking him, "Are you not the God in heaven, are you not the one who rules over all the kingdoms of the nation, are you not our God who drove out the inhabitants of this land before." 2nd Chronicles 20:6 -7(NKJV) the questions were rhetorical. He understood the power of God. In fact, Jehoshaphat wanted God to know that he is aware of his power and might, that he knows who God is and that he has faith in him! He even went as far as reminding God that Ammon, Moab, and Mount Seir were trying to take away what God had given to them. After the Israelites were told not to invade these people's land when the Israelites were in the wilderness traveling to the promise land.

"Now all Judah, with their little ones, their wives, and their children, stood before the LORD. Then the Spirit of the LORD came upon Jahaziel the son of Zechariah, the son of Benaiah, the son of Jeiel, the son of Mattaniah, a Levite of the sons of Asaph, in the midst of the assembly. And he said, "Listen, all you of Judah and you inhabitants of Jerusalem, and you, King Jehoshaphat!' Thus, says the LORD to

you: 'Do not be afraid nor dismayed because of this great multitude, for the battle is not yours, but Gods." 2nd Chronicles 20:13-15(NKJV)

Step Five: Jehoshaphat listened to the Lord! This is a famous quote, "Do not be afraid nor dismayed because of this great multitude, for the battle is not yours, but Gods." This is saying to pray to God and let God fight your battles.

"Tomorrow, go down against them. They will surely come up by the Ascent of Ziz, and you will find them at the end of the brook before the Wilderness of Jeruel. You will not need to fight in this battle. Position yourselves, stand still and see the salvation of the LORD, who is with you, O Judah and Jerusalem! Do not fear or be dismayed; tomorrow go out against them, for the LORD is with you." 2nd Chronicles 20:16-17 (NKJV)

Step Six: Jehoshaphat, after listening to the Lord, set a strategy or plan of action.

"Then the Levites of the children of the Kohathites and of the children of the Korahites stood up to praise the LORD God of Israel with voices loud and high. So, they rose early in the morning and went out into the Wilderness of Tekoa; and as they went out, Jehoshaphat stood and said, 'Hear me, O Judah and you inhabitants of Jerusalem: Believe in the LORD your God, and you shall be established; believe His prophets, and you shall prosper." 2nd Chronicles 20:19-20(NKJV)

Step Seven: Believe in the plan of action; know that God will straighten your path.

"And when he had consulted with the people, he appointed those who should sing to the LORD, and who should praise the beauty of holiness, as they went out before the army and were saying:

> *"Praise the LORD,*
> *For His mercy endures forever."*

Now when they began to sing and to praise, the LORD set ambushes against the people of Ammon, Moab, and Mount Seir, who had come against Judah; and they were defeated. For the people of Ammon and Moab stood up against the inhabitants of Mount Seir to utterly kill and destroy them. And when they had made an end of the inhabitants of Seir, they helped to destroy one another. So, when Judah came to a place overlooking the wilderness, they looked toward the multitude; and there were their dead bodies, fallen on the earth. No one had escaped. When Jehoshaphat and his people came to take away their spoil, they found among them an abundance of valuables on the dead bodies, and precious jewelry, which they stripped off for themselves, more than they could carry away; and they were three days gathering the spoil because there was so much. And on the fourth day they assembled in the Valley of Berachah, for there they blessed the LORD; therefore, the name of that place was called The Valley of Berachah until this day." 2nd Chronicles 20:21-26(NKJV)

Step Eight: With God's help, you can be successful! Again, with the help of God you can succeed.

"NOW FAITH IS THE SUBSTANCE OF THINGS HOPED FOR, THE EVIDENCE OF THINGS NOT SEEN"

Hebrews 11:1 (NKJV)

STEP FIVE

STEP OUT IN FAITH!

The concept of faith incorporates what we believe and how we stand by those beliefs. "Faith" is defined as complete trust or confidence in someone or something. It is the powerful belief in God or the doctrines of a religion that is based on spiritual understanding rather than proof. Hebrews 11:1 (NKJV) defines faith as ***"the substance of things hoped for, the evidence of things not seen."***

Faith is a lot like a muscle that you do not know is there until you go to use it. It was not until they stripped me of everything did I rely on my faith in God to help pull me through the dark times. Your faith is tested when you go through your trials and tribulations, which we will all experience in some forms or fashions. What is it we do when faced with trials? Do we run and hide, do we look the other way, or do we lean on the Lord for support while we walk through the fire? God wants us to lean on him.

Apostle Peter stated that faith must be tested. He also made other statements that we should consider. He said that we are shielded through faith given by the power of God which protects us. He informed us that we are born again through the hope we have in Jesus Christ, who died for us. That Jesus Christ provides a pathway to our inheritance, which is our salvation. He reminded us that our suffering is only for a little while, which not only refines who we are, but tests our strength.

In 1 Peter 1:3-7 (NIV), he says, ***"in his great mercy he has given us new birth into a living hope through the resurrection of Jesus Christ from the dead, and into an inheritance that can never perish, spoil or fade. This inheritance is kept in heaven for you, who through faith are shielded by God's power until the coming of the salvation that is ready to be revealed in the last time. In all this you greatly rejoice, though now for a little while you may have had to suffer grief in all kinds of trials. These have come so that the proven genuineness of your faith—of greater worth than gold, which perishes even though refined by fire—may result in praise, glory and honor when Jesus Christ is revealed."***

In the book of Luke, there is a story about a woman whose faith was demonstrated by the fact that she believed in Jesus Christ. She believed he could cure her, so in desperation, she touched him, and it cured her. Luke 8:43-48 (NKJV) says, ***"now a woman, having a flow of blood for twelve years, who had spent all her livelihood on physicians and could not be healed by any, came from behind and touched the border of his garment. And immediately her flow of blood stopped. And Jesus said, "Who touched me?" When all denied it, Peter and those with him said," Master, the multitudes throng and press You, and You say, Who***

Touched Me." But Jesus said, "somebody touched me, for I perceived power going out from me. Now when the woman seen that she was not hidden, she came trembling; and falling down before him, she declared to Him in the presence of all the people the reason she had touched him and how she was healed immediately. And he said to her, "Daughter, be of good cheer; your Faith has made you well. Go in peace."

The Bible lets us know that faith is all-encompassing, and that doubt can interfere with our faith. In fact, it says that doubt is like a wave of the sea. In James 1:6-8 (NIV), it says, ***"But when you ask, you must believe and not doubt, because the one who doubts is like a wave of the sea, blown and tossed by the wind. That person should not expect to receive anything from the Lord. Such a person is double-minded and unstable in all they do."***

It was not until I facilitated bible studies did I realize that many of the Prophets from the Old Testament were alluding to Jesus Christ in the form of a prophecy. It was their faith in action, their belief that the Messiah would come, even if not in their lifetime. He was coming. For example, the Prophet Isaiah prophesied that John the Baptist was going to come to prepare the way for Jesus Christ. Isaiah 40: 3-5 (NIV) states that ***"a voice of one calling: 'In the wilderness prepare the way for the Lord; make straight in the desert a highway for our God. Every valley shall be raised up, every mountain and hill made low; the rough ground shall become level, the rugged places a plain. And the glory of the Lord will be revealed, and all people will see it together. For the mouth of the Lord has spoken."*** The Prophet Malachi stated God will send a messenger to prepare a way. Malachi 4:5 (NIV) says, ***"I will send my messenger, who will prepare the way before me."***

THE POWER OF FAITH

In the book of Matthew, Jesus Christ surmised that just a little faith can move mountains. In the Parable of the Mustard Seed, he said, ***"The kingdom of heaven is like a mustard seed, which a man took and sowed in his field, which indeed is the least of all the seeds; but when it is grown, it is greater than the herbs and becomes a tree, so that the birds of the air come and nest in its branches."*** Matthew13:31-32 (NKJV). Jesus continued to use the analogy of a mustard seed by saying, **"Because of your unbelief; for assuredly, I say to you, if you have faith as a mustard seed, you will say to this mountain, 'Move from here to there,' and it will move; and nothing will be impossible for you."** Matthew 17:20 (NKJV)

There came a time when the Apostles of Jesus Christ said to Jesus, ***"Increase our Faith.*** [6] ***So the Lord said,*** **"If you have faith as a mustard seed, you can say to this mulberry tree, 'Be pulled up by the roots and be planted in the sea,' and it would obey you.** "Luke 17:5-6 (NKJV) That is what we should pray for right now, for our faith to be increased because certainly, we have mountains to move and roots to be planted!

The Apostle Paul wrote about "faith," in a manner that should make us to consider our own faith and the ability to pull through tough times. In Romans 5:1-5 (NKJV) he said, ***"Therefore, having been***

justified by faith, we have peace with God through our Lord Jesus Christ, through whom also we have access by faith into this grace in which we stand, and rejoice in hope of the glory of God. And not only that, but we also glory in tribulations, knowing that tribulation produces perseverance; and perseverance, character; and character, hope. Now hope does not disappoint, because the love of God has been poured out in our hearts by the Holy Spirit who was given to us."

Let's not forget about the story of Moses. Moses, standing on the water's edge, at the Red Sea, with the Israelites scared and vocal. The Egyptians with their mighty horses were coming, however, the Israelites could not see the Egyptians, but they could feel them coming. It was like an earthquake, getting closer with each second. Moses had absolute faith in God when he reached up to the sky with his rod and had the Red Sea part. It was miraculous and done with faith.

Exodus 14:21-31(MSG) says, ***"Then Moses stretched out his hand over the sea and GOD, with a terrific east wind all night long, made the sea go back. He made the sea dry ground. The seawaters split. The Israelites walked through the sea on dry ground with the waters on a wall to the right and to the left. The Egyptians came after them in full pursuit, every horse and chariot and driver of Pharaoh racing into the middle of the sea. It was now the morning watch. GOD looked down from the Pillar of Fire and Cloud on the Egyptian army and threw them into a panic. He clogged the wheels of their chariots; they were stuck in the mud.***

The Egyptians said, "Run from Israel! GOD is fighting on their side and against Egypt!" GOD said to Moses, "Stretch out your hand over the sea and the waters will come back over the Egyptians, over their chariots, over their horsemen." Moses stretched his hand out over the sea: As the day broke and the Egyptians were running, the sea returned to its place as before. GOD dumped the Egyptians in the middle of the sea. The waters returned, drowning the chariots and riders of Pharaoh's army that had chased after Israel into the sea. Not one of them survived.

But the Israelites walked right through the middle of the sea on dry ground, the waters forming a wall to the right and to the left. GOD delivered Israel that day from the oppression of the Egyptians. And Israel looked at the Egyptian dead, washed up on the shore of the sea, and realized the tremendous power that GOD brought against the Egyptians. The people were in reverent awe before GOD and trusted in GOD and his servant Moses."

We need to have faith that God will see us through this season of our lives.

"IF ANY OF YOU LACKS WISDOM, YOU SHOULD ASK GOD, WHO GIVES GENEROUSLY TO ALL WITHOUT FINDING FAULT, AND IT WILL BE GIVEN TO YOU"

James 1:5 (NKJV)

STEP SIX

PRAY FOR WISDOM AND SEEK GUIDANCE

God is your personal compass. Pray. Speak to God. Prayer is an intimate communication with God. It can contain a request for help, offer gratitude or be a personal conversation. The reasons for praying may vary. It is of utmost importance that you make your request to God for wisdom, knowledge and understanding, as well as the direction that you should take on issues affecting you. It can be in the form of supplication, kneeling and bending down, or meditating upon the word of God. Communicating with God through prayer builds a stronger relationship with him, yet it can provide guidance, understanding, praise, trust, faith, confession, repentance, etc. Prayer offers many benefits because of the Word of God:

a. God's Word is a Shield.
b. God's Word Bring Peace.
c. God's Promise is Fulfilling and Satisfying.
d. God's Word Allows for Personal Growth.
e. Rejoicing in God's Word Brings Glory to God.
f. God's Word Changes You.

The harder life becomes, the harder it is to pray. Depression, discouragement, and the feeling of being overwhelmed can cause you to turn your back on God. But that is when you must pray. Prayer is communicating with God. Just think, we were made in the image of God, by God, for his purpose. God wants a relationship with us, you and me. Therefore, we should pray to him at all times. Ephesians 6:18 states, ***"And pray in the Spirit on all occasions with all kinds of prayers and requests. With this in mind, be alert and always keep on praying for all the Lord's people."***

Sometimes, when I think of praying to God, I ask myself what should I say or what should I do? Do you have the same thought? Jesus Christ told his Disciples that they should not pray like hypocrites. That praying should not be repeating the same old line, in public, for all to see, as if you are proving your self-righteousness to others. It should be done in private. He can be trusted with our utmost secrets, desires, and fears. In Matthew 6:9-13 (NIV), Jesus Christ even provided the language that should be used when they prayed. He instructed them to say:

> ***"Our Father in heaven,***
> ***hallowed be your name,***
> ***your kingdom come,***
> ***your will be done,***
> ***on earth as it is in heaven.***
> ***Give us today our daily bread.***
> ***And forgive us our debts,***
> ***as we also have forgiven our debtors.***
> ***And lead us not into temptation,***
> ***but deliver us from the evil one."***

This language is very specific. The "Prayer" acknowledges the sacredness of God and that his will shall be done in heaven as well as earth. In fact, earth should become a duplicate of Heaven. God has and will provide our daily needs. He will forgive us as we have forgiven others. And we should pray that we are not tempted or deceived, but delivered from evil and sin of this world.

Many people read from the book of Psalms as their devotional scriptures because many of them are prayers that are put to music. The book of Psalms is a collection of songs, hymns, or poetry. The book itself is a collection of one hundred and fifty psalms. It is the longest book in the Bible. It contains the longest chapter, Psalm 119, with one hundred and seventy-six verses.

King David wrote most of the Psalms. You remember David. When he was a child, he took on the giant, the Philistine, Goliath, with a slingshot and then chopped off his head with the Philistine's own sword. From an early child, King David believed in God and the power of God, utilizing that belief by communicating with God. He prayed religiously. There came a time in which he was preparing to build the Temple, but God stopped him and told him that his son, Solomon, would build the Temple because he killed too many men. Yet, he wrote several pilgrimage songs, including Psalm 122, which is one of fifteen. It is a song that is sung while ascending Mount Sinai by those making the pilgrimage to pray and offer their sacrifices to God. On the surface, Psalm 122 is a beautiful, yet simple prayer. Psalm 122 (NKJV) states,

"A Song of Ascents. Of David.
I was glad when they said to me,
"Let us go into the house of the LORD."

Our feet have been standing
Within your gates, O Jerusalem!

Jerusalem is built
As a city that is compact together,

Where the tribes go up,
The tribes of the LORD,
To the Testimony of Israel,
To give thanks to the name of the LORD.

For thrones are set there for judgment,
The thrones of the house of David.

Pray for the peace of Jerusalem:
"May they prosper who love you.

Peace be within your walls,
Prosperity within your palaces."

For the sake of my brethren and companions,
I will now say, "Peace be within you."

Because of the house of the LORD our God
I will seek your good.

Can you imagine your best friend inviting you to their church for a special occasion? You look forward to it because you have heard all about the wonderful comings and goings about the Pastor, the choir, the Bible Study programs and their outreach ministry. You are excited to be a part of it. This is how the Pilgrims felt as they walked, climbed, hiked Mount Sinai. Excited to be there! Singing this song. Now you are there, in your friend's church. Your feet are standing in a sacred place. What is prayed for within this Psalm? Peace, both literal and figurative. This psalm mentions "peace" three times. Jerusalem to be at peace. Peace be within you. And peace be within your walls. Interpreting this psalm, we should pray for "peace." Yes, peace for Jerusalem. Internal peace for ourselves. And peace at home, where we live, where we work and where we visit.

I used to consider the way people prayed while I was at Church, Bible Study or just saying the grace before a meal. Were they long winded or to the point? Was it personal or more ritualistic? I have come to understand that praying can be anything that is acceptable to God, so long as you are communicating with him. There is a powerful one verse prayer in 1 Chronicles 4:10 (NIV), the Prayer of Jabez, which has become very popular. It says,

> ***"Jabez cried out to the God of Israel, "Oh, that you would bless me and enlarge my territory! Let your hand be with me, and keep me from harm so that I will be free from pain." And God granted his request.***

Although the Prayer of Jabez is short, it says so much. First, Jabez asked God to bless him. Second, he asked God to enlarge his territory. Third, he requested God stay with him or, better yet, allow him to stay in the presence of God. Fourth, he wanted God to keep him from harm. And fifth, he wanted to be free from pain. What Christian does not desire the same thing that Jabez' desired? Can you imagine with just a small prayer, so much of the heart could be conveyed? I had to ask myself whether I ever prayed such a short and powerful prayer. How about you? When was the last time you asked God to keep you from harm or to allow you to be pain free? This is quite an example of what should be prayed for by all of us.

Sometimes, when we do not know what to pray for, maybe we should simply express our gratitude to God for all that he has done for us. Hannah, the mother of Samuel, the Prophet, did not have children for many years, especially during her prime. She was married to Elkanah, and he had a second wife, Peninnah, who had children. She would torment Hannah until she cried. There came a time when their husband went up to town to worship and to offer a sacrifice. Their husband would give Hannah a double portion of the sacrificial meat because he loved her, but she was not satisfied. There came a time in which Hannah stood outside praying and crying to God, seeking a child of her own. Her lips would move, but her words could not be heard. The Prophet Eli thought she was drunk, but she told him no, that she was praying to God because she was distraught, she had no child. The Prophet Eli told her to go in peace for God will grant her request. In fact, that is exactly what occurred. Shortly thereafter, she became pregnant with her son, Samuel, whom she dedicated to God.

The reason this prayer is significant because of what she says to God after the birth of Samuel. In 1st Samuel 2, (NIV) she says,

"My heart rejoices in the LORD;
in the LORD my horn is lifted high.
My mouth boasts over my enemies,
for I delight in your deliverance.

"There is no one holy like the LORD;
there is no one besides you;
there is no Rock like our God.

"Do not keep talking so proudly
or let your mouth speak such arrogance,
for the LORD is a God who knows,
and by him deeds are weighed.

"The bows of the warriors are broken,
but those who stumbled are armed with strength.

Those who were full hire themselves out for food,
but those who were hungry are hungry no more.
She who was barren has borne seven children,
but she who has had many sons pines away.

"The LORD brings death and makes alive;
he brings down to the grave and raises up.

The LORD sends poverty and wealth;
he humbles and he exalts.

He raises the poor from the dust
and lifts the needy from the ash heap;
he seats them with princes
and has them inherit a throne of honor.
"For the foundations of the earth are the LORD's;
on them he has set the world.

He will guard the feet of his faithful servants,
but the wicked will be silenced in the place of darkness.
"It is not by strength that one prevails;

Those who oppose the LORD will be broken.
The Most High will thunder from heaven;
the LORD will judge the ends of the earth.
"He will give strength to his king
and exalt the horn of his anointed."

Hannah's prayer is significant for many reasons. She begins her prayer by rejoicing in God's grace and mercy. She shows her gratitude that her prayers had been answered. She is thankful that she has been delivered, which she boasts over her enemies. This is all in the first verse of her prayer.

Hannah acknowledges that there is only one true and living God. There is no one like him. He knows each of us by our deeds and desires. Hannah reminds us that the big, strong soldier can be broken down, while the weak could be built up. Telling us that those who are hungry, may hunger no more, while those who are satiated now, may become hungry again. That God has the power of life and death, wealth and poverty, etc. The poor and needy will sit at the throne of honor, his faithful servants will be guarded, and that God will judge the earth.

PERSONAL JOURNEY

Let me tell you about an incident involving prayer. I was not raised near my grandmother. I was raised in Cleveland, Ohio. My mother was from a little town called Pickens, Mississippi, about an hour north of Jackson, Mississippi. My grandmother did not visit often, but one year, she came to visit us. She shared my bedroom with me. One evening, I walked into my bedroom and found her bent over on the floor. Being a child, I thought something bad had happened. I panicked and hollered for my mother so she could come and help. My grandmother stopped me and told me she was praying.

Now that I am older, I find myself talking to God all the time. It is now that I am having sincere, heartfelt, and earnest prayers. I had to lose everything to truly consider the roles of God, Jesus Christ, and the Holy

Spirit in my life. I do not get down on my knees like I did when I was younger. My personal joke is that if I get down on the ground, I will definitely need a crane to get me up! Now, before I facilitate Bible Studies, I will get on my knees to pray for wisdom, direction, and that all the participants will learn something new or consider an issue from a different angle. Sometimes, after my prayer, I feel so certain of God's presence. It is peculiar. It is as if someone turned on the light!

I am afraid of praying in public. I am a private person, anyway. A loner, as it were. I was asked to close Bible Study by doing the closing prayer. I panicked. I recited the Lord's Prayer and requested that everyone joined me. It was not heartfelt, nor was it personal. Jesus Christ told his disciples to pray in that manner, which should have made it sufficient. Knowing how uncomfortable it was for me, my mother told me what she learned over the years. She relied upon a formula for public prayer that she was given in one of her many bible classes. It is A. C. T. S:

A - Adoration
C - Confession
T - Thanksgiving
S - Supplication

Public prayer is unnecessary for most of us; however, personal prayer is a requirement. The Bible speaks of "Prayer," and the benefits of prayer extensively. It lets us know we must ask God for help. In fact, James 5:13-16 (ESV) says that if a person is suffering, they should pray to the Lord. The "Prayer of Faith," says, ***"Is anyone among you suffering? Let him pray. Is anyone cheerful? Let him sing praise. Is anyone among you***

sick? Let him call for the elders of the church, and let them pray over him, anointing him with oil in the name of the Lord. And the prayer of faith will save the one who is sick, and the Lord will raise him up. And if he has committed sins, he will be forgiven. Therefore, confess your sins to one another and pray for one another, that you may be healed. The prayer of a righteous person has great power as it is working."

WHEN YOU DO NOT KNOW HOW TO PRAY, TALK!

It is believed that the Apostle Paul wrote thirteen books in the New Testament, including Romans. Originally, his name was Saul, and he persecuted Christians, including the Prophet Stephen. He was converted on the road to Damascus. Yet, he expanded the Church and provided various principles for the body of Christ to follow. He provided the "Good News" far and wide. He was imprisoned several times. Chased out of cities and towns. He also wrote some of the most inspiring works. In the book of Romans, the Apostle Paul lets us know that even if we do not know how to pray, the Holy Spirit will assist us. He said, ***"Likewise, the Spirit helps us in our weakness. For we do not know what to pray for as we ought, but the Spirit himself intercedes for us with groanings too deep for words. And he who searches hearts knows what is 'the mind of the Spirit,' because the Spirit intercedes for the saints according to the will of God. And we know that for those who love God, all things work together for good for those who are called according to his purpose. For those whom he foreknew, he also predestined to be conformed to the image of his Son, in order that he might be the firstborn among many***

brothers. And those whom he predestined he also called, and those whom he called he also justified, and those whom he justified he also glorified." Romans 8:26-30 (ESV)

MAKE THE REQUEST, PRAY FOR HELP

Jesus taught his Disciples the Lord's Prayer after they requested to be taught how to pray. They said, ***"Lord, teach us to pray, as John also taught his disciples."*** (Luke 11:1)(NIV) Jesus told his Disciples to ask whatever they wished, and it will be done. John 15:7-11(NIV) says, ***"If you abide in me, and my words abide in you, ask whatever you wish, and it will be done for you. By this my Father is glorified, that you bear much fruit and so prove to be my disciples. As the Father has loved me, so have I loved you. Abide in my love. If you keep my commandments, you will abide in my love, just as I have kept my Father's commandments and abide in his love. These things I have spoken to you, that my joy may be in you, and that your joy may be full."***

Continue to Pray

We are told to continue to pray to God ***"pray without ceasing."*** 1 Thessalonians 5:17 (NKJV). In Luke 11:9-13 (NKJV), we are told to keep asking, seeking, and knocking. In fact, Jesus speaking to his Disciples said, ***"So I say to you, ask, and it will be given to you; seek, and you will find; knock, and it will be opened to you. For everyone who asks receives, and he who seeks finds, and to him who knocks it will be opened. If a son asks for bread from any father among you, will he give him a stone? Or***

if he asks for a fish, will he give him a serpent instead of a fish? Or if he asks for an egg, will he offer him a scorpion? If you then, being evil, know how to give good gifts to your children, how much more will your heavenly Father give the Holy Spirit to those who ask Him!"

PRAY FOR SPIRITUAL STRENGTH

The Bible talks about the necessity of praying for spiritual strength, especially when we are going through trials and tribulations. The Apostle Paul wrote in his letter to the Ephesians that they should pray for spiritual strength. He said, ***"For this reason I bow my knees before the Father, from whom every family in heaven and on earth is named that according to the riches of his glory he may grant you to be strengthened with power through his Spirit in your inner being, so that Christ may dwell in your hearts through faith—that you, being rooted and grounded in love, may have strength to comprehend with all the saints what is the breadth and length and height and depth, and to know the love of Christ that surpasses knowledge, that you may be filled with all the fullness of God. Now to him who is able to do far more abundantly than all that we ask or think, according to the power at work within us, to him be glory in the church and in Christ Jesus throughout all generations, forever and ever. Amen."*** Ephesians 3:14-21 (ESV)

PRAYER AT WORK

There are so many wonderful human beings in the Bible who prayed to God, including David. The story of David and King Saul can be found in 1 Samuel 29. David had been on the run from King Saul, who was jealous of David and for many years, he chased him with the intent of killing him. David had a relationship with God, remaining obedient and listening to him. David sought guidance from God through prayer. In fact, David had an opportunity to seek revenge against King Saul for all he had done to him. First, King Saul came into a cave to relieve himself. Not knowing that David and his men were hiding in that very same cave. David cut a small piece of King Saul's garment. Second, King Saul was asleep among his soldiers when David and his men quietly entered their area, taking some of their belongings. David refused to kill or even hurt King Saul because God anointed him.

Eventually tired of running, David decided to move his men and their families to an area that was controlled by the Philistines, called Ziklag. King Saul would never come in the land of the Philistines; they were enemies of the Israelites. David lived in the area for some time and had a good relationship with the King of the Philistines, King Achish. In fact, King Achish asked David and his men to join forces against the Israelites in Aphek. He agreed to do so.

While passing in the rear of the men with King Achish, the commanders of the Philistines said, ***"What are these Hebrews doing here?"*** 1 Samuel 29:3 (NKJV) Referring to David and his men. Achish said that it indeed was David. Continuing in 1 Samuel 29:4-5 (NIV), the

Commanders of the Philistines were concerned about the presence of David. *"But the commanders of the Philistines were angry with him. And the commanders of the Philistines said to him, "Send the man back, that he may return to the place to which you have assigned him. He shall not go down with us to battle, lest in the battle he become an adversary to us. For how could this fellow reconcile himself to his lord? Would it not be with the heads of the men here? Is not this David, of whom they sing to one another in dances?***

> ***'Saul has struck down his thousands,***
> ***and David his ten?"***

Achish acknowledged David had been honest and righteous, but David and his men could not take part in the battle against the Israelites. Achish told David to return to their homes, telling him, ***"Now then rise early in the morning with the servants of your lord who came with you, and start early in the morning, and depart as soon as you have light." So, David set out with his men early in the morning to return to the land of the Philistines."*** 1 Samuel 29:10-11 (NIV)

After their three-day journey back to Ziklag, David and his men realized that their town had been raided. ***"The Amalekites had made a raid against the Negeb and against Ziklag. They had overcome Ziklag and burned it with fire and taken captive the women and all who were in it, both small and great. They killed no one but carried them off and went their way. And when David and his men came to the city, they found it burned with fire, and their wives and sons and daughters taken captive. Then David and the people who were with him raised their***

voices and wept until they had no more strength to weep. David's two wives also had been taken captive, Ahinoam of Jezreel and Abigail the widow of Nabal of Carmel. And David was greatly distressed, for the people spoke of stoning him, because all the people were bitter in soul, each for his sons and daughters." 1 Samuel 30:1-6 (ESV)

After David's home was burned down, his town was raided, everyone was taken including his wives and children, his own men were threatening to "stone him," he prayed to God. ***"But David strengthened himself in the LORD his God."*** David turned to the Lord. ***"And David inquired of the LORD, 'Shall I pursue after this band? Shall I overtake them?' He answered him, 'Pursue, for you shall surely overtake and shall surely rescue.' So, David set out, and the six hundred men who were with him . . ."*** (1 Samuel 30 8-9)(ESV)

David and his men eventually caught up to the Amalekites. ***"Behold, they were spread abroad over all the land, eating and drinking and dancing, because of all the great spoil they had taken from the land of the Philistines and from the land of Judah. And David struck them down from twilight until the evening of the next day, and not a man of them escaped, except four hundred young men, who mounted camels and fled. David recovered all that the Amalekites had taken, and David rescued his two wives. Nothing was missing, whether small or great, sons or daughters, spoil or anything that had been taken. David brought back all."*** (1 Samuel 30 16-19)(ESV) When God is for you, who can be against you?

WE MUST PRAY!

The significance of the story is that we must pray to the Lord for direction, wisdom, knowledge, etc., or we are doomed to fail. Matthew 6:5-8 (NIV) states, ***"And when you pray, you must not be like the hypocrites. For they love to stand and pray in the synagogues and at the street corners, that they may be seen by others. Truly, I say to you, they have received their reward. But when you pray, go into your room and shut the door and pray to your Father who is in secret. And your Father who sees in secret will reward you. "And when you pray, do not heap up empty phrases as the Gentiles do, for they think that they will be heard for their many words. Do not be like them, for your Father knows what you need before you ask him."***

Let's Pray!

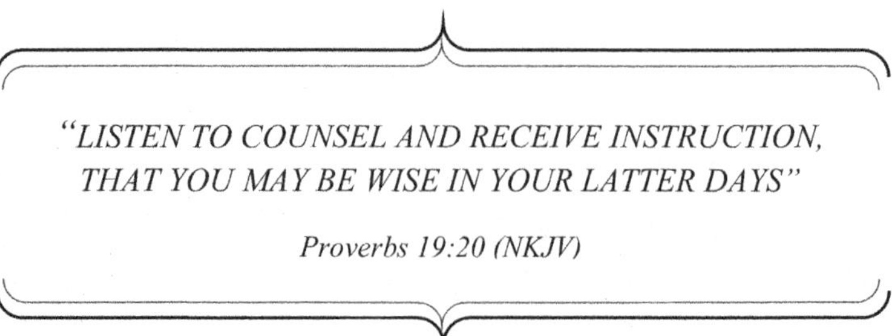

"LISTEN TO COUNSEL AND RECEIVE INSTRUCTION, THAT YOU MAY BE WISE IN YOUR LATTER DAYS"

Proverbs 19:20 (NKJV)

STEP SEVEN

LISTEN AND WAIT ON GOD

Listen for God's word. This requires the act of being attentive and focusing on him. Distractions can stand in the way of your ability to hear and understand the word of God. Listening to him differs from hearing your children, your parents or your spouse. You must allow yourself to be in a peaceful environment or calm state of mind because he speaks in different ways, which may include coincidences, those things that are uncanny and unexplained. He expresses his plan through individuals such as friends, family, sermons, counseling, chance encounters, etc. He communicates through dreams. His plan may be shown by a closed door or opened window.

I have heard it argued that God has been trying to get our attention, but we have refused to listen. I do not know about that rationale. However, I think it is important to take time out, allowing ourselves to re-evaluate our circumstances. This can be an opportunity to set new goals and to reflect on the past. Determine what is valuable and reassess life. We are so busy with the day-in and day-out tasks and chores of life that it is nearly impossible to just stop. The Covid-19 pandemic has caused many of us to stop; to change our routine, to stay close to home. This is a time to listen to God.

It is necessary to listen and wait for God's answer to our prayers instead of plowing ahead. Proverbs 18:13 (NKJV) says, ***"He who answers a matter before he hears it, it is folly and shame to him."*** Proverbs 19:27 (NKJV) says, ***"Cease listening to instruction, my son, and you will stray from the words of knowledge."*** When you listen and wait for God's answer, you will be successful. Proverbs 19: 20-21 (NKJV) states that those that listen to God's Counsel will stand. It says, ***"Listen to counsel and receive instruction, that you may be wise in your latter days. There are many plans in a man's heart, nevertheless the LORD's counsel—that will stand."***

Proverbs, the Second Chapter, contains verses that state that if you receive God's word, understanding and discernment will follow and grow within you. The entire chapter speaks about the expansion of wisdom through the receipt of God's word. Proverbs 2:1-6 (NIV) provides benefits of listening for the word of God:

> ***"My son, if you receive my words,***
> ***And treasure my commands within you,***
> ***So that you incline your ear to wisdom,***
> ***And apply your heart to understanding.***
> ***Yes, if you cry out for discernment,***
> ***And lift up your voice for understanding,***
> ***If you seek her as silver,***
> ***And search for her as for hidden treasures.***

Then you will understand the fear of the LORD,
And find the knowledge of God.
For the LORD gives wisdom;
From His mouth come knowledge and understanding."

GOD IS TRYING TO GET OUR ATTENTION

From the time we were created, God has been trying to get our attention. His methods have been a bit odd. The Prophet Ezekiel was made to lie on each side in front of the temple for Three Hundred and Ninety Days. He cooked his food using human poop/dung as the fuel. Ezekiel 4:9–12 (NKJV) states, ***"Also take for yourself wheat, barley, beans, lentils, millet, and spelt; put them into one vessel, and make bread of them for yourself. During the number of days that you lie on your side, three hundred and ninety days, you shall eat it. And your food which you eat shall be by weight, twenty shekels a day; from time to time you shall eat it. You shall also drink water by measure, one-sixth of a hin; from time to time you shall drink. And you shall eat it as barley cakes; and bake it using fuel of human waste in their sight."***

The Prophet Isaiah walked around Jerusalem naked and barefoot for three years. Isaiah 20:3-6 (NKJV) states, ***"Then the LORD said, 'Just as My servant Isaiah has walked naked and barefoot three years for a sign and a wonder against Egypt and Ethiopia, so shall the king of Assyria lead away the Egyptians as prisoners and the Ethiopians as captives, young and old, naked and barefoot, with their buttocks uncovered, to the shame of Egypt. Then they shall be afraid and ashamed of Ethiopia, their expectation and Egypt, their glory. And the inhabitant of this territory will say in that day, 'Surely such is our***

expectation, wherever we flee for help to be delivered from the king of Assyria; and how shall we escape?"

The Prophet Hosea was forced to marry a harlot, a prostitute. He had children with her, too. Their names were "Unloved" and "Not-My-People." Hosea was imitating God. He led his family, while God led the Israelites. Both defiled and imperfect people. Hosea 1:1 (NKJV) says, ***"When the LORD began to speak by Hosea, the LORD said to Hosea:***

> ***"Go, take yourself a wife of harlotry***
> ***And children of harlotry,***
> ***For the land has committed great harlotry***
> ***By departing from the LORD."***

The Prophet Jeremiah wore a linen sash but could not put it in water. He hid it in a hole under a rock near the Euphrates River, where it deteriorated before he was made to wear it as a symbol of the ruined pride of the people of Israel who refused to listen to God. In Jeremiah 13:1-11 (MSG), ***"GOD told me, 'Go and buy yourself some linen shorts. Put them on and keep them on. Don't even take them off to wash them.' So, I bought the shorts as GOD directed and put them on. Then GOD told me, 'Take the shorts that you bought and go straight to Perath and hide them there in a crack in the rock.' So, I did what GOD told me and hid them at Perath. Next, after quite a long time, GOD told me, 'go back to Perath and get the linen shorts I told you to hide there.' So, I went back to Perath and dug them out of the place where I had hidden them. The shorts by then had rotted and were worthless. GOD explained, 'this is the way I am going to ruin the pride of Judah and the great pride of Jerusalem—a wicked bunch of people who won't obey me, who do only***

what they want to do, who chase after all kinds of no-gods and worship them. They're going to turn out as rotten as these old shorts. Just as shorts clothe and protect, so I kept the whole family of Israel under my care' — GOD's Decree — "so that everyone could see they were my people, a people I could show off to the world and be proud of. But they refused to do a thing I said."

Refusing to Listen to God has Consequences

Not only does the Bible provide examples of people who didn't listen to God, but it also tells us stories about people who heard God but refused to comply or be obedient to him. In 1 Samuel 8, the Israelites wanted a king, just like some of the surrounding territories. *(Even then, people were trying to keep up with the Joneses.)* Prior to their desire for a King, the Israelites went through a period of time when they were governed by Judges, hence the book of Judges, but that did not go well at all. They wanted a King. Not realizing or understanding that God was their King. The Prophet Samuel discussed their request with God, who told him to tell the people about the dangers of a King.

In 1 Samuel 8:10-18 (NKJV), Prophet Samuel said, ***"And Samuel told all the words of the LORD to the people that asked of him a king. And he said, This will be the manner of the king that shall reign over you: He will take your sons, and appoint them for himself, for his chariots, and to be his horsemen; and some shall run before his chariots. And he will appoint him captains over thousands, and captains over fifties; and will set them to ear his ground, and to reap his harvest,***

and to make his instruments of war, and instruments of his chariots. And he will take your daughters to be confectionaries, and to be cooks, and to be bakers. And he will take your fields, and your vineyards, and your olive groves, even the best of them, and give them to his servants. And he will take the tenth of your seed, and of your vineyards, and give to his officers, and to his servants. And he will take your menservants, and your maidservants, and your best young men, and your asses, and put them to his work. He will take the tenth of your sheep: and you shall be his servants. And you shall cry out in that day because of your king which you shall have chosen you; and the LORD will not hear you in that day."

The Israelites not only disregarded God as their King, but upon learning of what would occur if they became a Kingdom under the rule of a King, they still desired a King. They were willing to follow a man with limited insight and wisdom instead of an all-knowing God. This is an example of hearing the word of God but following your own path. God gave the Israelites a King as requested. And his warning became the way of life.

The book of Jeremiah contains fifty-two chapters, of which the majority provides one singular warning insisting that the Israelites change their behavior to avoid God's wrath. The people refused to listen, although Jeremiah tried various methods, including breaking pots, wearing a ruined sash around his waist, etc., to get their attention. Jeremiah 2:1-3(ESV) says, ***"The word of the LORD came to me, saying, "Go and proclaim in the hearing of Jerusalem, thus says the LORD,***

"I remember the devotion of your youth,
your love as a bride,
how you followed me in the wilderness,
in a land not sown.
Israel was holy to the LORD,
the firstfruits of his harvest.
All who ate of it incurred guilt;
disaster came upon them,
declares the LORD."

The warnings continue to the Faithless. God's anger and wrath had been ignited. Repent and change before punishment takes place. Jeremiah 3:11-12(ESV) says, ***"And the LORD said to me, "Faithless Israel has shown herself more righteous than treacherous Judah. Go, and proclaim these words toward the north, and say,***

"Return, faithless Israel,
declares the LORD.
I will not look on you in anger,
for I am merciful,
declares the LORD;
I will not be angry forever."

Truth had perished. It was unrecognizable. Jeremiah 7:28-29 (ESV) says, ***"And you shall say to them, 'This is the nation that did not obey the voice of the LORD their God and did not accept discipline; truth has perished; it is cut off from their lips.***

"Cut off your hair and cast it away;
raise a lamentation on the bare heights,
for the LORD has rejected and forsaken
the generation of his wrath."

Deception was the law of the day. Jeremiah 8:4-5 (ESV) says, ***"You shall say to them, thus says the LORD:***

> ***"When men fall, do they not rise again?***
> ***If one turns away, does he not return?***
> ***Why then has this people turned away***
> ***in perpetual backsliding?***
> ***They hold fast to deceit;***
> ***they refuse to return."***

The Israelites had to be refined and tested through their punishment. Jeremiah 9:7-8 (ESV) says, ***"Therefore thus says the LORD of hosts:***

> ***"Behold, I will refine them and test them,***
> ***for what else can I do, because of my people?***
> ***Their tongue is a deadly arrow;***
> ***it speaks deceitfully;***
> ***with his mouth each speaks peace to his neighbor,***
> ***but in his heart he plans an ambush for him."***

The Israelites were reminded of their creator. Jeremiah 10:11 (ESV) says, ***"Thus shall you say to them: "The gods who did not make the heavens and the earth shall perish from the earth and from under the heavens."***

They were given an opportunity to consider the covenants of their forefathers. Jeremiah 11:3-5(ESV) says, ***"You shall say to them, Thus, says the LORD, the God of Israel: Cursed be the man who does not hear the words of this covenant that I commanded your fathers when I brought them out of the land of Egypt, from the iron furnace,***

saying, listen to my voice, and do all that I command you. So, shall you be my people, and I will be your God, that I may confirm the oath that I swore to your fathers, to give them a land flowing with milk and honey, as at this day." Then I answered, "So be it, LORD."

God told them they will be taken from their lands. Jeremiah 12:14 (ESV) says, ***"Thus says the LORD concerning all my evil neighbors who touch the heritage that I have given my people Israel to inherit: "Behold, I will pluck them up from their land, and I will pluck up the house of Judah from among them."***

Droughts and other plagues will take place. Jeremiah 14:1 (ESV) says, ***"The word of the LORD that came to Jeremiah concerning the drought. . ."***

The Israelites will go through various types of pestilence, famine, and captivity. Jeremiah 15:1-2 (ESV) says, ***"Then the LORD said to me, "Though Moses and Samuel stood before me, yet my heart would not turn toward this people. Send them out of my sight and let them go! And when they ask you, 'Where shall we go?' you shall say to them, 'Thus says the LORD:***

> ***"Those who are for pestilence, to pestilence,***
> ***and those who are for the sword, to the sword;***
> ***those who are for famine, to famine,***
> ***and those who are for captivity, to captivity."***

They will be a people in mourning. Jeremiah 16:5 (ESV) says, ***"For thus says the LORD: Do not enter the house of mourning, or go to lament or grieve for them, for I have taken away my peace from this people, my steadfast love and mercy, declares the LORD."***

The word of God was given to the Israelites at the gates of Judah and Israel. Jeremiah 17:19-20 (ESV) says, ***"Thus said the LORD to me: "Go and stand in the People's Gate, by which the kings of Judah enter and by which they***

go out, and in all the gates of Jerusalem, and say: 'Hear the word of the LORD, you kings of Judah, and all Judah, and all the inhabitants of Jerusalem, who enter by these gates."

The power is in the hand of the Potter reminding the Israelites of their creator. Jeremiah 18:5-6 (ESV) says, ***"Then the word of the LORD came to me: "O house of Israel, can I not do with you as this potter has done? Declares the LORD. Behold, like the clay in the potter's hand, so are you in my hand, O house of Israel."***

Punishment for the inequities is at hand, repent and turn back to God. Jeremiah 19:3 (ESV) says, ***"You shall say, 'Hear the word of the LORD, O kings of Judah and inhabitants of Jerusalem. Thus, says the LORD of hosts, the God of Israel: Behold, I am bringing such disaster upon this place that the ears of everyone who hears of it will tingle."***

The last step was on Prayer and Request for Help. This step states you must Listen and Wait on the Lord.

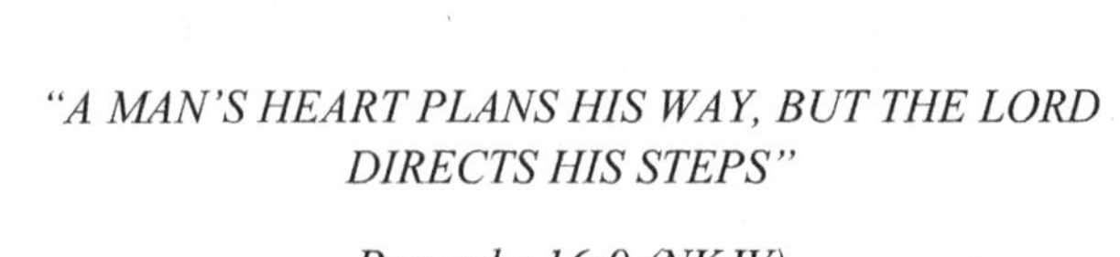

"A MAN'S HEART PLANS HIS WAY, BUT THE LORD DIRECTS HIS STEPS"

Proverbs 16:9 (NKJV)

STEP EIGHT

SET UP A "JOY" PLAN

A "Joy" Plan is a plan of action that is purposely seeking to bring joy to your life by taking actions that will uplift you, change your attitude, and help you grow as a person. Let us list some possibilities:

- Reminiscing with Friends about the Good Ole Days
- Taking a Drive to the Water's Edge or Taking in the Fall Foliage
- Writing Down your Dreams and Hopes
- Reading Inspirational and Encouraging Stories
- Participating in a Bible Class
- Taking a Class Online
- Making an Apple Pie, any pie, from Scratch
- Planting Flowers in the Garden or in a Pot on your Windowsill
- Volunteering your time at the Local Animal Shelter
- Volunteering your time at the Women's Shelter
- Assisting your favorite Political Candidate
- Listening to Your Favorite Artist on YouTube
- Listening to Sermons Online
- Looking at Old Photos
- Volunteering at the Food Bank or Meals-on-Wheels
- Writing a Book

- Getting a list of the "Sick and Shut-In" from your Church and calling to offer encouragement
- Going to a Concert, seeing Live Entertainment
- Taking a Trip, a Weekend Getaway
- Visiting Friends and Family
- Babysitting the Children of your Family members and Friends

Now, you may say to yourself that these activities appear to be "light" on the "Joy" category, but they are activities that get you away from your own thoughts and allow you to be more open to possibilities that include helping someone else, having contact with others, and developing additional relationships and human contact.

Now, your "Joy" plan does not have to be limited to those items on the above list. Whatever makes you happy should be included. Prior to Covid-19, my "Joy" plan included quarterly plan. I loved seeing live performances. Sometimes, I would go to free events or I would plan to see my favorite artists. Many times, I would go by myself and I usually meet strangers who become friends. I also loved to travel, so each quarter, I would schedule a trip, whether it was close to home or far away. This allowed me to change my scenery and also my state of mind.

I must admit, I needed a time out from my life. I purposely scheduled a "Joy" plan. It was personal to me. I realized I was going through the motions of life, but not really present with purpose. For example, I would wake up, shower, get dressed, take my vitamins, and get in my car. But mentally, I would still be asleep. I wouldn't know if I felt the water on my back when I took the shower or the taste of the vitamins, even the chewable vitamin C, which is extremely tart. Sometimes, I would ask myself whether I took a shower. But for the smell of the perfume, I would not remember. Other times, I would drive down the road and I would ask myself; how did I get here, literally. Almost as if I had just woken up, and then driving down the road!

I came up with the idea of a joy plan after my primary care physician put me on anti-depressants and anti-anxiety medicine. Years ago, when I was separating from my husband, I went through a time in which I was very depressed and did not seem to snap out of it. I went to a doctor who said, "Not until you change your circumstances, will you change for the better!" Years later, I realized that if my circumstance is going to change, I must make that change.

LIFE TRANSITIONS

When I was young, I was different than I am now. I grew up in a traditional household; both my father and my mother were present, and they both loved me. I was sheltered in a way suburban kids with wealthy parents are sheltered. I did not have an enemy in the world. I roller skated, played kick ball, rode my bike, ran between the neighbors' houses and had fun. No care in the world. When I enrolled in Ohio State National Guards as a military police officer, I was disciplined for being "too" familiar with the upper ranks, with no respect for rank. Everyone was a friend.

But I changed and did not realize it. When was the last time I had a "hearty" laugh, not a giggle, but laughed until I cried? When was the last time I saw a band play or some live entertainment that made me holler until my voice was hoarse the next day? When was the last time I read a romantic novel and just fell in love with the characters? My life was one of going to court or to the office in the morning, meeting with clients in the afternoon, writing pleadings or preparing schedules in the evening, leaving to see my father at the nursing home, stopping by to see my mother before she went to bed, coming home to have a quick exchange with my spouse and rubbing the dog. Yes, I changed.

SOMETHING DIFFERENT

Years ago, when I was in the mortgage business, I would keep a note for myself which stated, "PLAN YOUR WORK AND WORK YOUR PLAN!" I did not make this quote up nor did I know who did, but it is true.

You need to make a "Joy" plan. You may be sitting down and reading this book and saying to yourself, "Hasn't she heard we are in the midst of a pandemic?" Or better yet, you may think, "I am broke, I just spent my last dollar on this book for encouragement and direction. How does she think I am going to make a "Joy" Plan?" A joy plan does not have to cost you money, but it requires that you consider your needs and dedicate some time for you.

During this period of Covid-19, the livelihoods of many individuals have been changed. Their business may have been adversely affected, they may have been laid off indefinitely, their employers may have closed shop, or their restaurants have limited service or carryout only with little, if any, gratuities paid. This is a season of change. We have to plan accordingly, but now, this is not forever! Amid this crisis, you still must think of yourself. Not just your safety, but your joy.

WHAT DOES THE BIBLE SAY ABOUT PLANNING?

The Bible has many names for planning and setting goals; the "call of God," the "will of God," "mission," or "vision," to name a few. Let us look at some of the bible verses pertaining to planning. I want to begin with Proverbs 6:6-8 (ESV) because it says even an "ant" plans her work. It says, ***"Go to the ant, O sluggard; consider her ways, and be wise. Without having any chief, officer, or ruler, she prepares her bread in summer and gathers her food in harvest."***

The Bible specifically states that when you are preparing your "plans," seek God's guidance first. Proverbs 3:5-6 (ESV) says, ***"trust in the LORD with all your heart, and do not lean on your own understanding. In all your ways acknowledge him, and he will make straight your paths."*** Proverbs 16:9 (ESV) *says,* ***"The heart of man plans his way, but the LORD establishes his steps."*** It also states in Proverbs 15:22 (ESV) that, ***"Without counsel plans fail, but with many advisers they succeed."*** The Bible requires that you seek God's guidance because tomorrow is not guaranteed, in fact, James 4:13-15 (ESV) states, ***"Come now, you who say, "Today or tomorrow we will go into such and such a town and spend a year there and trade and make a profit" - yet you do not know what tomorrow will bring. What is your life? For you are a mist that appears for a little time and then vanishes. Instead, you ought***

to say, "If the Lord wills, we will live and do this or that." So, it is necessary to Plan, but seek God's guidance in the Planning.

Remember, your plans should become a road map to assist in reaching your goals, so write them down and consider each step. Proverbs 24:27 (ESV) states, ***"Prepare your work outside; get everything ready for yourself in the field, and after that build your house."*** In the Book of Luke, there is an analogy given as to building a tower without the necessary supplies or going to war without the necessary men. Luke 14:28-33 (ESV) states, ***"For which of you, desiring to build a tower, does not first sit down and count the cost, whether he has enough to complete it? Otherwise, when he has laid a foundation and is not able to finish, all who see it begin to mock him, saying, 'This man began to build and was not able to finish.' Or what king, going out to encounter another king in war, will not sit down first and deliberate whether he is able with ten thousand to meet him who comes against him with twenty thousand? And if not, while the other is yet a great way off, he sends a delegation and asks for terms of peace. So therefore, any one of you who does not renounce all that he has cannot be my disciple."***

Sometimes, it takes time to develop a plan. It may not be immediate, but the Bible says for us not to be anxious. In Matthew 6:25-34 (ESV), it says that not only are we not to be anxious, but to seek the kingdom of God first:

> ***"Therefore, I tell you, do not be anxious about your life, what you will eat or what you will drink, nor about your body, what you will put on. Is not life more than***

> ***food, and the body more than clothing? Look at the birds of the air: they neither sow nor reap nor gather into barns, and yet your heavenly Father feeds them. Are you not of more value than they? And which of you by being anxious can add a single hour to his span of life? And why are you anxious about clothing? Consider the lilies of the field, how they grow: they neither toil nor spin, yet I tell you, even Solomon in all his glory was not arrayed like one of these. But if God so clothes the grass of the field, which today is alive and tomorrow is thrown into the oven, will he not much more clothe you, O you of little faith? Therefore, do not be anxious, saying, 'What shall we eat?' or 'What shall we drink?' or 'What shall we wear?' For the Gentiles seek after all these things, and your heavenly Father knows that you need them all. But seek first the kingdom of God and his righteousness, and all these things will be added to you. "Therefore, do not be anxious about tomorrow, for tomorrow will be anxious for itself. Sufficient for the day is its own trouble."***

The Bible tells us that a good plan, leads to success. Psalm 20:4 (NIV) states, ***"May he give you the desire of your heart and make all your plans succeed."*** 2 Chronicles 15:7 (NIV) states, ***"But as for you, be strong and do not give up, for your work will be rewarded."*** Psalm 33:11 (NIV) says, ***"But the plans of the Lord stand firm forever, the***

purposes of his heart through all generations." Success comes from a "successful," plan.

Do you remember the story of Joseph from Genesis? Let me do a quick recap if you do not remember. Jacob had twelve sons. Now, Jacob, who was later called Israel, loved Joseph more than all his children, because he *was* the son of his old age. Joseph had received dreams from God. He saw that his family would praise him, and he told his brothers of his dreams. Joseph's brothers grew jealous and conspired against him to kill him. First, they placed Joseph in a pit, but his brother, Judah, had a rethink about the idea of killing him. Judah said, ***"What profit is there if we kill our brother and conceal his blood"*** (Genesis 37:26) (ESV) He advised they should sell him to the Ishmaelites and his brothers listened.

Potiphar, an officer of Pharaoh, captain of the guard, an Egyptian, bought him from the Ishmaelites and saw that the LORD *was* with him and that the LORD made all he did to prosper in his hand. Potiphar put Joseph over his house. And it came to pass that Potiphar's wife desired Joseph, stating, "lay with me," but he refused. She later accused Joseph of sexual impropriety and he was imprisoned.

While imprisoned, the King of Egypt imprisoned his Butler and the Baker. They each had a dream, and both of them sought Joseph's help in interpreting their dream. One would be restored, and one would die. The one that would be restored agreed to remember Joseph. Then it came to pass, at the end of two full years, that Pharaoh had a dream. No one could interpret his dream. Finally Joseph was brought before Pharaoh to interpret his dream.

Joseph said that there would be great prosperity for seven years, followed by a great famine for seven years. Then Pharaoh said to Joseph, "Inasmuch as God has shown you all this, *there is* no one as discerning and wise as you. You shall be over my house, and all my people shall be ruled according to your word; only in regard to the throne will I be greater than you."

Now, this is not the end of the story of Joseph, but I want to stop right here. Joseph developed a plan of action that saved not only his family, but the entire area by thorough planning:

· The problem had to be understood.
· He needed a vision and a strategy.
· The right people had to be put in place.
· They had to be obedient.
· Someone had to make sure it was all operating according to plan.
· The work had to be measured.

Finally, your plan must be strategic. But do not forget, you must remember that God has a plan and purpose for you, so be encouraged. Jeremiah 29:11 (ESV) states, ***"for I know the plans I have for you, declares the LORD, plans for welfare and not for evil, to give you a future and a hope."***

"FOR HE HIMSELF HAS SAID,
"I WILL NEVER LEAVE YOU NOR FORSAKE YOU"

Hebrews 13:5 (NKJV)

STEP NINE
EXPECT A BLESSING

A "Blessing" is God's favor and protection. It can come in many forms, including physical and spiritual blessings. A physical blessing is one that pertains to our physical being. They include the provisions God gives in the form of food, drink, and shelter so that we can maintain a safe and secure life. God gives us food. ***"He gives food to every creature"*** Psalm 136:25(NIV). God gives us drink. ***"Come, all you who are thirsty, come to the waters; and you who have no money, come, buy and eat! Come, buy wine and milk without money and without cost"*** Isaiah 55:1 (NIV). God gives us shelter. ***"Those who go to God Most High for safety will be protected by the Almighty. I will say to the Lord, "You are my place of safety and protection"*** Psalm 91:1-2 (NCV).

We can receive spiritual blessings. Spiritual blessings are those things God gives us for our spiritual being. It is a term expressing the fullness of blessing in God's gift of eternal life in Jesus Christ. In the book of Ephesians 1:3 (ESV), we are told that God has blessed us in Christ with every spiritual blessing, ***"Blessed be the God and Father of our Lord Jesus Christ, who has blessed us in Christ with every spiritual blessing in the heavenly places."*** While during this life, the Spirit gives its fruit. Galatians 5:22-23 (ESV) says, ***"But the fruit of the Spirit is love, joy, peace, patience, kindness, goodness, faithfulness, gentleness, self-control; against such things there is no law."***

I know you are probably wondering why I have included "expect a blessing" as a separate step, separate from "step out in faith." Most people think they are the same thing, but they are not the same. Faith is the complete trust in someone or something. While expectation is a firm belief that something is going to happen. For Christians, they expect to be blessed by God. For example, my faith allows me to believe that Jesus Christ died on the cross for me, that he was the living sacrifice, that if I accept Jesus Christ, I will receive salvation as well as the Holy Spirit. That is my faith. However, I expect my soul to go to heaven. That is my expectation. Now, my faith is an assumption or an underlying principle for my expectations. They certainly go hand-in-hand and faith comes before expectation.

Let me give you an example of faith and expectation in an ordinary situation. I purchased a 2018 Volkswagen Tiguan a couple of years ago. When the service engine light comes on, I take it to the local Volkswagen dealership for service. I have faith that the mechanics will service my car properly and I expect to drive away from the dealership with no problems.

Several years ago, I read a book by Norman Vincent Peale called, "The Power of Positive Thinking." Mr. Peale surmised that your attitude affects your outcome. If you had an affirming attitude, you would have a successful outcome. Likewise, if your attitude was negative, failure would be the outcome. In his book, he told stories of various people he had encountered proving just his point. People with difficult circumstances which were almost impossible to overcome were successful despite their issues because of their expectation, their belief, that they would achieve their goal. Their optimistic beliefs altered their course, but when you are disappointed or disillusioned, it is hard to be positive.

When we are going through trials and tribulations, it is difficult to be upbeat, to think positive and to believe that you are entitled to the desired outcome when so much is negative. We do not even realize that what we are thinking has become a hindrance to the result we desire. It is time for a change. We must recognize that we may determine our own negative outcome. Therefore, we have to guard our thoughts and expect a blessing! Romans 12:2 (ESV) says, ***"Do not be conformed to this world, but be transformed by the renewal of your mind, that by testing you may discern what is the will of God, what is good and acceptable and perfect."*** Philippians 4:13 (ESV) says, ***"I can do all things through him who strengthens me***." Proverbs 4:23 (ESV) states, ***"Keep your heart with all vigilance, for from it flow the springs of life."***

STORY OF BALAK AND BALAAM, THE UNKNOWN BLESSING

I would like to discuss a story that speaks to being blessed by God. But in this case, the receiver of God's blessing, the Israelites, was unaware that they were being blessed. They had an expectation to arrive at the land promised to them by God, yet they were oblivious to the blessings provided by God. I wanted to include this story because many of us do not realize our many blessings because we can only see life through the lenses of our circumstances. But we are being blessed.

The story begins with the Israelites getting closer to the promise land. They needed to go through other kingdoms to arrive at the promise land and sought permission from the various kings. In the case at hand, it was Sihon, king of the Amorites, who said no to the passage and lost their land to the Israelites in a battle. Numbers 21:21-24 (NKJV), ***"Then Israel sent messengers to Sihon king of the Amorites, saying, 'Let me pass through your land. We will not turn aside into fields or vineyards; we will not drink water from wells. We will go by the King's Highway until we have passed through your territory.' But Sihon would not allow Israel to pass through his territory. So Sihon gathered all his people together and went out against Israel in the wilderness, and he came to Jahaz and fought against Israel. Then Israel defeated him with the edge of the sword and took possession of his land . . ."***

As the Israelites conquered various kingdoms, the neighboring kingdoms grew fearful that their lands would be taken by them too. The Israelites were resting near Jericho. Numbers 22:1 (NKJV) state,

"Then the children of Israel moved, and camped in the plains of Moab on the side of the Jordan across from Jericho."

Unbeknownst to the Israelites, there was a battle brewing that could seriously harm them. The King of the Moabites believed they would overthrow his kingdom because of the sheer size of the Israelites. Numbers 22:2-4 (NKJV) continues by saying, ***"Now Balak, who was King of the Moabites, the son of Zippor saw all that Israel had done to the Amorites. And Moab was exceedingly afraid of the people because they were many, and Moab was sick with dread because of the children of Israel. So Moab said to the elders of Midian, "Now this company will lick up everything around us, as an ox licks up the grass of the field."***

They hatched a plan to curse the Israelites. Balak hired a Prophet, Balaam, the son of Beor at Pethor, to curse the Israelites. King Balak said, ***"Look, a people has come from Egypt. See, they cover the face of the earth, and are settling next to me! Therefore, please come at once, curse this people for me, for they are too mighty for me. Perhaps I shall be able to defeat them and drive them out of the land, for I know that he whom you bless is blessed, and he whom you curse is cursed." "So, the elders of Moab and the elders of Midian departed with the diviner's fee in their hand, and they came to Balaam and spoke to him the words of Balak."*** Numbers 22:5-7(NKJV)

Balaam spoke to the elders and asked them to stay the night while he prayed. God told Baalam not to go. ***"And God said to Balaam, 'You shall not go with them; you shall not curse the people, for they are blessed.' So, Balaam rose in the morning and said to the***

princes of Balak, 'Go back to your land, for the LORD has refused to give me permission to go with you.' Then Balak again sent princes, more numerous and more honorable than they. And they came to Balaam and said to him, 'Thus says Balak the son of Zippor: 'Please let nothing hinder you from coming to me; for I will certainly honor you greatly, and I will do whatever you say to me. Therefore, please come, curse this people for me." Numbers 22:12-17(NKJV)

Balaam reluctantly refused to go to curse the Israelites. But he said he would pray to God, again. ***"Then Balaam answered and said to the servants of Balak, 'Though Balak were to give me his house full of silver and gold, I could not go beyond the word of the LORD my God, to do less or more. Now therefore, please, you also stay here tonight, that I may know what more the LORD will say to me."*** Numbers 22:18-19(NKJV)

God gave Balaam a conditional approval to go. ***"And God came to Balaam at night and said to him, 'If the men come to call you, rise and go with them; but only the word which I speak to you—that you shall do."*** Numbers 22:20 (NKJV)

God grew angry with Balaam. He said "no" to Balaam for the first time. He meant "no." Yet, Balaam asked again. God gave him a conditional approval to go, but still grew angry sending an Angel to Balaam. An Angel that the Donkey of Balaam could see clearly. ***"Then God's anger was aroused because he went, and the Angel of the LORD took His stand in the way as an adversary against him. And he was riding on his donkey, and his two servants were with him. Now the donkey saw the Angel of the LORD standing in the way with His drawn***

sword in His hand, and the donkey turned aside out of the way and went into the field. So, Balaam struck the donkey to turn her back onto the road. Then the Angel of the LORD stood in a narrow path between the vineyards, with a wall on this side and a wall on that side. And when the donkey saw the Angel of the LORD, she pushed herself against the wall and crushed Balaam's foot against the wall; so, he struck her again. Then the Angel of the LORD went further and stood in a narrow place where there was no way to turn either to the right hand or to the left. And when the donkey saw the Angel of the LORD, she laid down under Balaam; so, Balaam's anger was aroused, and he struck the donkey with his staff." Numbers 22:22-27 (NKJV)

The Donkey spoke to Balaam: ***"Then the LORD opened the mouth of the donkey, and she said to Balaam, 'What have I done to you, that you have struck me these three times? And Balaam said to the donkey, 'Because you have abused me. I wish there were a sword in my hand, for now I would kill you!' So, the donkey said to Balaam, 'Am I not your donkey on which you have ridden, ever since I became yours, to this day? Was I ever disposed to do this to you?' And he said, "No."*** Numbers 22:28-30 (NKJV)

Balaam never considered the fact that he was speaking with the Donkey, but he soon realized the Angel of the Lord was present. ***"Then the LORD opened Balaam's eyes, and he saw the Angel of the LORD standing in the way with His drawn sword in His hand; and he bowed his head and fell flat on his face. And the Angel of the LORD said to him, 'Why have you struck your donkey these three times? Behold, I have come out to stand against you, because your way***

is perverse before me. The donkey saw Me and turned aside from Me these three times. If she had not turned aside from me, surely, I would also have killed you by now, and let her live.' And Balaam said to the Angel of the LORD, 'I have sinned, for I did not know You stood in the way against me. Now therefore, if it displeases you, I will turn back. Then the Angel of the LORD said to Balaam, 'Go with the men, but only the word that I speak to you, that you shall speak.' So, Balaam went with the princes of Balak." Numbers 22:31-35 (NKJV)

Balaam told Balak to build seven altars, prepare seven bulls and seven rams as burned offerings, to prepare for the curse on the Israelites. Numbers 23:1 continues, ***"Then Balaam said to Balak, 'Build seven altars for me here, and prepare for me here seven bulls and seven rams.' And Balak did just as Balaam had spoken, and Balak and Balaam offered a bull and a ram on each altar. Then Balaam said to Balak, 'Stand by your burnt offering, and I will go; perhaps the LORD will come to meet me, and whatever He shows me I will tell you.' So, he went to a desolate height. And God met Balaam, and he said to Him, 'I have prepared the seven altars, and I have offered on each altar a bull and a ram.' Then the LORD put a word in Balaam's mouth, and said, "Return to Balak, and thus you shall speak." So, he returned to him, and there he was, standing by his burnt offering, he and all the princes of Moab."*** Numbers 23:1-6 (NKJV)

Balaam blessed the Israelites instead of cursing them in opposition to the request of Balak:

"And he took up his oracle and said:

"Balak the king of Moab has brought me from Aram,
From the mountains of the east.
'Come, curse Jacob for me,
And come, denounce Israel!'
"How shall I curse whom God has not cursed?
And how shall I denounce whom the LORD has not denounced?"
Numbers 23:7-8 (NKJV)

Balak, upset with Balaam, but believing that maybe God was limited by jurisdiction, moved to an area that they knew the people to follow a pagan God. ***"So, he brought him to the field of Zophim, to the top of Pisgah, and built seven altars, and offered a bull and a ram on each altar. And he said to Balak, "Stand here by your burnt offering while I meet the LORD over there." Then the LORD met Balaam, and put a word in his mouth, and said, "Go back to Balak, and thus you shall speak." So, he came to him, and there he was, standing by his burnt offering, and the princes of Moab were with him. And Balak said to him, "What has the LORD spoken?"*** Numbers 23:14-17 (NKJV)

Balaam blesses the Israelites:

"Then he took up his oracle and said:

"Rise up, Balak, and hear!
Listen to me, son of Zippor!
"God is not a man, that He should lie,
Nor a son of man, that He should repent.
Has He said, and will He not do?
Or has He spoken, and will He not make it good?
Behold, I have received a command to bless;

He has blessed, and I cannot reverse it."
Numbers 23:18-20 (NKJV)

Balak told Balaam, if you cannot curse the Israelites, certainly do not bless them. Balaam reminded Balak that he must do all that God tells him to do.***"Then Balak said to Balaam, "Neither curse them at all, nor bless them at all!" So, Balaam answered and said to Balak, "Did I not tell you, saying, 'All that the LORD speaks, that I must do'?"*** Numbers 23:25-26 (NKJV)

Believing that if Balak took Balaam to an area where he could not see the Israelites, that their chances of succeeding with cursing the Israelites would be better, so the third attempt, went like this: ***"Now when Balaam saw that it pleased the LORD to bless Israel, he did not go as at other times, to seek to use sorcery, but he set his face toward the wilderness. And Balaam raised his eyes, and saw Israel encamped according to their tribes; and the Spirit of God came upon him."*** Numbers 24:1-2 (NKJV)

For the third time, Balaam blessed the Israelites,

"Then he took up his oracle and said:

"The utterance of Balaam the son of Beor,
The utterance of the man whose eyes are opened,
The utterance of him who hears the words of God,
Who sees the vision of the Almighty,
Who falls down, with eyes wide open:
"How lovely are your tents, O Jacob!
Your dwellings, O Israel!
Like valleys that stretch out,
Like gardens by the riverside,

Like aloes planted by the LORD,
Like cedars beside the waters." Numbers 24:3-6 (NKJV)

Balaam ended by saying, ***"Blessed is he who blesses you. And cursed is he who curses you."*** Numbers 24:9 (NKJV)

Balak was thoroughly angry at Balaam. Instead of cursing the Israelites, Balaam blessed them three times. ***"Then Balak's anger was aroused against Balaam, and he struck his hands together; and Balak said to Balaam, "I called you to curse my enemies, and look, you have bountifully blessed them these three times! Now therefore, flee to your place. I said I would greatly honor you, but in fact, the LORD has kept you back from honor."*** Numbers 24:10-11 (NKJV)

Now, Balaam actually prophesied the coming of Jesus Christ as well as the destruction of Moab. ***"So, he took up his oracle and said:***

"The utterance of Balaam the son of Beor,
And the utterance of the man whose eyes are opened;
The utterance of him who hears the words of God,
And has the knowledge of the Most High,
Who sees the vision of the Almighty,
Who falls down, with eyes wide open:
"I see Him, but not now;
I behold Him, but not near;
A Star shall come out of Jacob;
A Scepter shall rise out of Israel,
And batter the brow of Moab,
And destroy all the sons of tumult." Numbers 24:15-17(NKJV)

These events transpired because the Israelites were traveling to the Promised Land. Not only did they get the Promised Land, but the lands that were on the way. However, the Israelites did not know at the time that Balak was seeking to curse them.

The Israelites had faith in God. They traveled in the wilderness seeking the Promised Land. They expected to arrive at the Promised Land, which they did, but they also were blessed with other property along the way.

We must expect a blessing, even if we do not know how it will arrive!

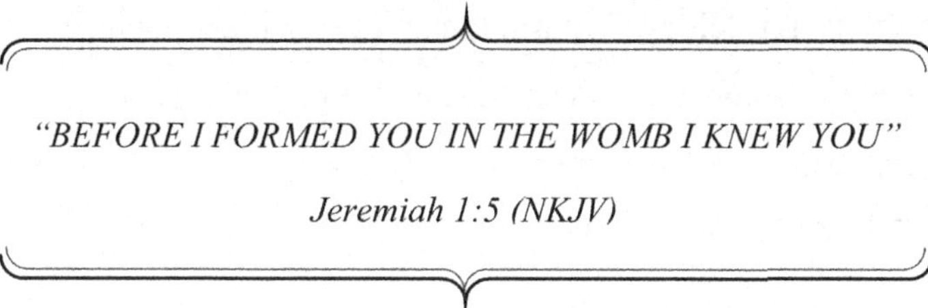

"BEFORE I FORMED YOU IN THE WOMB I KNEW YOU"

Jeremiah 1:5 (NKJV)

STEP TEN
WHAT IS YOUR VALUE?

There are various methods used to carry out business valuation, real estate, stocks, bonds, etc., but how do we value ourselves? How we see ourselves will determine our value. Professional title or employment does not determine worth, and neither do skill sets, experiences, or history. What we offer our friends and family as emotional, psychological or physical support may create value, but it does not determine it. Even when we compare ourselves to someone else, we cannot arrive at it. Therefore, value is not how we compare to someone else, but how we compare to ourselves. Awareness and acceptance of our strengths, weaknesses, experiences, history and other characteristics confer benefit to the people close to us. However, we seek to place a price tag on our value, but when something is absolutely priceless, how can financial worth be assessed?

When I wrote this question in my outline, I initially thought, what a silly question. Each of us has our own identity, name, history, and experiences. Could we have our own identity, yet be undefined? I remember when I broke up with my very first boyfriend, my first love, I was totally lost. It felt as if a part of me was missing, no longer there. Even though it was almost forty-years ago, I still remember thinking that I became a shadow of my former self. I knew what he loved to eat. I knew what he enjoyed doing. I knew what made him mad. I knew what made him laugh. But what made me laugh?

People would ask me when I was young, “What do you want to be when you grow up?” Sometimes, I ask young people the same question. The answer is invariably a title or position. For example, I want to be a doctor, a nurse, a lawyer, a dentist, a business owner, an astronaut, etc. I have always been okay with that answer until now. I have reflected on that question and realized that there is an underlying assumption you are defined by your employment, your title, your position, etc. This assumption concludes you are only as valuable as your employment, the money that you make to keep the roof over your head, food on your table, clothes on your back, etc. When a person is defined by their position, title and/or income, who do they become when they are no longer employed?

From March through August 2020, Marketplace.org stated that approximately thirty-one million people were receiving some form of unemployment, meaning they did not have their regular employment. Numerous businesses were slated to close. People who were working were not working their normal schedules. Food Pantries and other charitable organizations were inundated with people who needed help. The Centers for Disease Control (CDC) published an article on August 14, 2020, called, “Mental Health, Substance Use, and Suicidal Ideation During the Covid-19 Pandemic–United States” which stated that 40% of the adults in the United States reported struggling with some form of mental health or substance abuse. It said that 11% of adults considered suicide; 31% suffered from anxiety or depression; 26% suffering with trauma or stress-related event and 13% increased their use of various types of substances. This is all during Covid-19. Prior to Covid-19, Wikipedia stated that suicide is a major national public health issue in the United States. The country has one of the highest suicide rates among wealthy nations.

I have counseled some people who felt lost and alone. They were going through a critical situation, and no one else seemed to notice. They felt worthless. I have observed young women whose fathers were not present in their life seek attention from men who did not hold them in high esteem. I have also witnessed people, including myself, give too much of themselves to others, seeking their approval. The goal is usually to seek someone or something else before themselves. "Second Position Mentally" is what I have called it. What is important or the value of oneself is not readily apparent. I have asked myself many times, what am I worth? Better yet, do I have any value?

This is what I have learned. The scarcer a commodity, the more valuable it is! For example, the clearer, bright and large diamond cost more than the diamonds that have imperfections, discolored and small. In fact, the diamonds that are clear, bright, and large are harder to find, causing them to be rare, and causing their value to be higher. Now, there is only one of you with all of your strengths and weaknesses. There will never be a second one of you. Since there is only one of you, what should be your value? Priceless. It is my belief that to value yourself based on your title, income, or position is a fool's folly that leaves us unsatisfied, unfulfilled, and useless. Yet, our society tells us we must pay to play. Our value comes from God, not man. He considered us so valuable that he sent his only begotten son to live among men, die on the cross for our sins, and three days later, he was resurrected. He sent the Comforter and gave salvation to those who have faith in him. Just think about that. We must be valuable for such a sacrifice.

THE WORDS OF KING SOLOMON

King Solomon wrote the book of Ecclesiastes. He had Seven Hundred Wives and Three Hundred Concubines. He was fabulously wealthy and wise; the king of the United Kingdom of Israel who succeeded his father, King David. He wrote everything was meaningless. In Ecclesiastes 1:8-9 (NIV), it says, ***"The eye never has enough of seeing, nor the ear its fill of hearing. What has been will be again, what has been done will be done again; there is nothing new under the sun."*** I believe that this is a warning to stop chasing those things that man has made. He described a hamster on its wheel, going around and around but not becoming any better. For example, when have you heard a billionaire say that they have had enough money and that they are going to stop making money? King Solomon was rich. He had silver and gold, but it was *"meaningless."*

King Solomon had wisdom, but at a certain point, even that was *"meaningless."* Continuing in Ecclesiastes 1:12-15 (NIV), it states, ***"I, the Teacher, was king over Israel in Jerusalem. I applied my mind to study and to explore by wisdom all that is done under the heavens. What a heavy burden God has laid on mankind! I have seen all the things that***

are done under the sun; all of them are meaningless, a chasing after the wind. What is crooked cannot be straightened; what is lacking cannot be counted."

King Solomon lamented pleasures were meaningless. ***"Come now, I will test you with pleasure to find out what is good." But that also proved to be meaningless. "Laughter," I said, "is madness. And what does pleasure accomplish?" I tried cheering myself with wine and embracing folly—my mind still guiding me with wisdom. I wanted to see what was good for people to do under the heavens during the few days of their lives."*** Ecclesiastes 2:1-3 (NIV)

King Solomon stated God must be the answer in the search for fulfillment. ***"A person can do nothing better than to eat and drink and find satisfaction in their own toil. This too, I see, is from the hand of God, for without him, who can eat or find enjoyment? To the person who pleases him, God gives wisdom, knowledge and happiness, but to the sinner he gives the task of gathering and storing up wealth to hand it over to the one who pleases God. This too is meaningless, a chasing after the wind."*** Ecclesiastes 2:24-26 (NIV)

He concluded by saying that you should remember God while you are young, before your season of trials and tribulations, because a day will come when there will be no pleasure. Be focused on God.

> ***"Now all has been heard;***
> ***here is the conclusion of the matter:***
> ***Fear God and keep his commandments,***
> ***for this is the duty of all mankind.***
> ***For God will bring every deed into judgment,***

including every hidden thing,
whether it is good or evil." Ecclesiastes 12:13-14 (NIV)

THE WOMAN AT THE WELL

There is a story in the Bible about a Samaritan woman by a well. This woman's circumstances, both personally and professionally, determined her status in her community. Some argue that she was a prostitute. The Bible says she is a Samaritan. First, they considered her a mixed-breed or mixed-race person. After the Assyrians conquered Samaria, they resettled on that land with foreigners. Those people intermarried with the Israelites in the region. The foreigners also brought their pagan gods. The Jews accused the Samaritans of idolatry. Second, the Samaritans furthered the rift by producing their own version of the Pentateuch, the five books of Moses. These books included Genesis, Exodus, Leviticus, Numbers, and Deuteronomy. And third, the Samaritans wanted to worship at Shechem, on Mount Gerizim, where it had been in the time of Joshua. The Jews, however, built their first temple in Jerusalem.

This woman had no value in the society. In fact, the story began with her alone at the well, with no other woman present to keep her company. It appeared as if she was ostracized. When Jesus Christ came to the well and spoke to her, Jesus Christ not only acknowledged seeing her, but that he "knows" her. For him, she has value, the same value as a rich man, today. She was so affirmed by what Jesus Christ said to her, she ran and told others, bringing them to Jesus Christ. What is the value of saving souls? The answer has to be priceless!

In John 4:5-30 (NCV), it says, ***"In Samaria Jesus came to the town called Sychar, which is near the field Jacob gave to his son Joseph. Jacob's well was there. Jesus was tired from his long trip, so he sat down beside the well. It was about twelve o'clock noon. When a Samaritan woman came to the well to get some water, Jesus said to her, 'Please give me a drink.' This happened while Jesus' followers were in town buying some food. The woman said, "I am surprised that you ask me for a drink, since you are a Jewish man, and I am a Samaritan woman." Jewish people are not friends with Samaritans.***

Jesus said, "If you only knew the free gift of God and who it is that is asking you for water, you would have asked him, and he would have given you living water." The woman said, "Sir, where will you get this living water? The well is very deep, and you have nothing to get water with. Are you greater than Jacob, our father, who gave us this well and drank from it himself, along with his sons and flocks?" Jesus answered, "Everyone who drinks this water will be thirsty again, but whoever drinks the water I give will never be thirsty. The water I give will become a spring of water gushing up inside that person, giving eternal life." The woman said to him, "Sir, give me this water so I will never be thirsty again and will not have to come back here to get more water."

Jesus told her, "Go get your husband and come back here." The woman answered, "I have no husband." Jesus said to her, "You are

right to say you have no husband. Really, you have had five husbands, and the man you live with now is not your husband. You told the truth." The woman said, "Sir, I can see that you are a prophet. Our ancestors worshiped on this mountain, but you say that Jerusalem is the place where people must worship."

Jesus said, "Believe me, woman. The time is coming when neither in Jerusalem nor on this mountain will you actually worship the Father. You Samaritans worship something you don't understand. We understand what we worship because salvation comes from the Jews. The time is coming when the true worshipers will worship the Father in spirit and truth, and that time is here already. You see, the Father too is actively seeking such people to worship him. God is spirit, and those who worship him must worship in spirit and truth." The woman said, "I know that the Messiah is coming." (Messiah is the One called Christ.) "When the Messiah comes, he will explain everything to us."

Then Jesus said, "I am he, I, the one talking to you." Just then his followers came back from town and were surprised to see him talking with a woman. But none of them asked, "What do you want?" or "Why are you talking with her?" Then the woman left her water jar and went back to town. She said to the people, "Come and see a man who told me everything I ever did. Do you think he might be the Christ?" So, the people left the town and went to see Jesus."

This story lets us know we are more than our circumstances and our experiences; however, they help to tell our story.

THE PERSONAL CHASE

Years ago, I was married to a proud and strategic black man from Mobile, Alabama. When I met him, he was charming, intelligent and a go-getter. He worked as a Chief Operating Officer for a small company in Northern Virginia. There came a time when a new Chief Executive Officer was hired, the company asked my spouse to train him. Later, that person left that position and they hired another person. Again, my spouse was asked to train her for the new role. Now, my spouse clearly knew what they expected of the person in that position because he had to train those given the position and he had to work hand-in-hand with them. In fact, he applied for the position several times. He would receive the pay, but not the title. He believed it was because he was black. His frustration was so intense; he would come home and tell me he quit his job. The first time he told me he quit his job, I panicked. The second time he told me he quit his job, I questioned him. And the third time he told me he quit his job, I accepted it because he did indeed quit his job.

After a period of uncertainty, he was hired in a new position, receiving almost a third of what he received from his previous job, but he received stock options, even though the company had not gone public. His office was near the owner's office and other corporate leaders. He developed a plan. He said that he would get to the office before the owner and other corporate leaders, and he would stay after they had gone home. Many of them would pass his office as they came and went. He received recognition in the form of more responsibility, better titles and more stock options.

There came a time when we had money in the bank, a large house in Great Falls, Virginia which was showcased in a magazine, a boat at the pier in the Gang Plank Marina in Washington, DC, and cars in the driveway. He became a drug addict. I was depressed. We were chasing the wrong things.

UNDERSTANDING OUR IDENTITY

The more we value possessions and pleasure, the less we value those things that truly define who we are as a person. Matthew 6:24 (NIV) says, ***"No one can serve two masters. Either you will hate the one and love the other, or you will be devoted to the one and despise the other. You cannot serve both God and money."*** Our value system cannot be based on what society has told us that matters the most, i.e., that car, that house, those clothes, etc. Our value begins with the family, even our adopted family. We are the daughter or son of our parents, our grandparents. This is the tree from which we were formed. Without it, our identity is harder to establish. Sometimes, I will watch a television show called "Paternity Court." Every so often, they would have an adult child trying to establish the identity of their father. Invariably, they would say, "I want to know who I belong to" and they would continue by stating that they feel "incomplete" without this determination. The desire to be whole is sometimes impalpable. Yet, many of us take our families for granted.

The Lord said in Jeremiah 1:5 (NIV) ***"Before I formed you in the womb, I knew you, before you were born, I set you apart; I appointed you as a prophet to the nations."*** My assistant brought pictures of an ultrasound which showed the growth of her grandson in her daughter's womb. She was waiting for his birth. She wanted to meet him, to determine what type of person he would become. I looked at the ultrasound pictures. They were not exactly clear, but it was not a complete blur. You could see the baby's head, baby's body, arms and legs forming into a person. A person who may be tall or short, skinny or fat, light or dark. Someone who would grow up to love long walks in the moonlight, picnics at the beach, or a long airplane ride to an exotic destination. But, in the womb, the Lord knows him and has set him apart!

THE BIBLE AND OUR IDENTITY

Our identity shall not come from the world, but from God. The Apostle Paul, who became a prolific follower of Jesus Christ and formed many churches, wrote thirteen books in the New Testament including Ephesians, which was one of the four books called the prison epistles, including Philippians, Philemon, and Colossians. In Ephesians, he discussed the "new" identity of Christians. First, he said that God chose us through Jesus Christ. Second, he gave us "glorious grace." He died for our sins; he was a living sacrifice, which was a transition from the Old Testament to the New Testament. Third, he redeemed us and forgave us of our sins. Fourth, he provides wisdom and knowledge as to the mystery of his will. Fifth, he will unite all things in him from both heaven and earth.

Sixth, we will obtain an inheritance. And seventh, the Holy Spirit indwells within us.

There is a wonderful passage about who we are in the eyes of God. In Ephesians 1:4-14 (NLT), it says, ***"Even before he made the world, God loved us and chose us in Christ to be holy and without fault in his eyes. God decided in advance to adopt us into his own family by bringing us to himself through Jesus Christ. This is what he wanted to do, and it gave him great pleasure. So, we praise God for the glorious grace he has poured out on us who belong to his dear Son. He is so rich in kindness and grace that he purchased our freedom with the blood of his Son and forgave our sins. He has showered his kindness on us, along with all wisdom and understanding."***

"God has now revealed to us his mysterious will regarding Christ—which is to fulfill his own good plan. And this is the plan: At the right time he will bring everything together under the authority of Christ - everything in heaven and on earth. Furthermore, because we are united with Christ, we have received an inheritance from God, for he chose us in advance, and he makes everything work out according to his plan."

"God's purpose was that we, Jews, who were the first to trust in Christ, would bring praise and glory to God. And now you, Gentiles, have also heard the truth, the Good News that God saves you. And when you believed in Christ, he identified you as his own by giving you the Holy Spirit, whom he promised long ago. The Spirit is God's guarantee that he will give us the inheritance he promised and that he has

purchased us to be his own people. He did this so we would praise and glorify him.

GIFT OF THE HOLY SPIRIT

Have you considered what it means to have the gift of the Holy Spirit? The gift of the Holy Spirit is that which is in you that causes you to seek a closer relationship with God. Along with our salvation, through faith in God comes the Holy Spirit. It possesses all the attributes of a personality. Keep in mind, personality exists wherever there's intelligence and reason and mind. The Holy Spirit is our teacher, leading us to the grace and mercy of God. (Nehemiah 9:20)(NIV) He offers us clarity of mind, giving us the ability to understand the word of God and to grow wiser. (Isaiah 11:2)(NIV) He gives us the power to discern the truth. (John 14:17)(NIV) He has many names in the Bible.

The Bible talks about God, his son, Jesus Christ, and the Holy Spirit. Yet the Holy Spirit is a person distinct from God the Father and God the Son. It was not until I learned the word that I understood the significance of the Holy Spirit. As Jesus prepared for his death, he spoke with his Disciples. He stated it was better for them if he continued his mission, including dying on the cross because he was sending a Helper, a Comforter. In John 14:15-17 (NLT), Jesus said, *"**If you love me, obey my commandments. And I will ask the Father, and he will give you another Advocate, who will never leave you. He is the Holy Spirit, who leads into all truth. The world cannot receive him because it isn't looking for him***

and doesn't recognize him. But you know him because he lives with you now and later will be in you."

Jesus told them that the Holy Spirit will not only help them, but teach them of all things, John 14:26 (NKJV) says, ***"But the Helper, the Holy Spirit, whom the Father will send in my name, he will teach you all things and bring to your remembrance all that I have said to you."*** The purpose of the Holy Spirit was varied. In Luke 4:17-19 (NLT) it states, ***"the scroll of Isaiah the prophet was handed to him. He unrolled the scroll and found the place where this was written:***

> ***"The Spirit of the LORD is upon me,***
> ***for he has anointed me to bring Good News to the poor.***
> ***He has sent me to proclaim that captives will be released,***
> ***that the blind will see,***
> ***that the oppressed will be set free,***
> ***and that the time of the LORD's favor has come."***

The anointing of the Holy Spirit helped bring the Good News to the poor. This was significant because the means of communicating were so different from methods of today. In order to bring the good news, the followers of Christ had to go to the people. They could not call, text, or email. The Holy Spirit assisted with equality and fairness in the community, not just the Church, seeking the release of captives and freeing the oppressed. It helped those that were blind to Jesus Christ and those who actually could not see because it gave the power to heal.

The Apostle Paul continued with what Jesus Christ said by stating that the Holy Spirit will help us in our weakness. The Holy Spirit will intercede on our behalf. Romans 8:26-30 (NLT) says, ***"And the Holy Spirit helps us in our weakness. For example, we don't know what God wants***

us to pray for. But the Holy Spirit prays for us with groanings that cannot be expressed in words. And the Father who knows all hearts knows what the Spirit is saying, for the Spirit pleads for us believers in harmony with God's own will. And we know that God causes everything to work together for the good of those who love God and are called according to his purpose for them. For God knew his people in advance, and he chose them to become like his Son, so that his Son would be the firstborn among many brothers and sisters. And having chosen them, he called them to come to him. And having called them, he gave them right standing with himself. And having given them right standing, he gave them his glory."

It is said that the Holy Spirit was given as a way to regenerate or renew according to God's mercy. ***"But when the kindness and the love of God our Savior toward man appeared, not by works of righteousness which we have done, but according to His mercy He saved us, through the washing of regeneration and renewing of the Holy Spirit, whom He poured out on us abundantly through Jesus Christ our Savior, that having been justified by His grace we should become heirs according to the hope of eternal life."*** Titus 3:4-7 (NKJV)

GIFT OF PEACE

The gift of "peace" is needed more today than ever before. I think about the meaning of peace. Is peace simply a conflict free existence? Is peace the same thing as tranquility? Is peace simply a state of mind? When I was growing up, my mother always said she needed "peace and quiet." I knew she meant she did not want to be disturbed. But as I grew older, I realized that peace means several things. For me, "peace" means that my mind can be free of conflicts, including dreams, fears, and thoughts that will cause my mind to be restless and on alert. For example, I want our country to be free of war and conflict, whether it is internal or international. We spend much of our time contemplating what will happen next. Peace could mean how to simply stay in the moment.

Jesus told his Disciples that he was not only going to send the Holy Spirit, but Peace. He said it's not the type of peace the world gives, but the type of Peace that can calm a troubled heart. In John 14:27 -31 (NLT), it says, "**I am leaving you with a gift - peace of mind and heart. And the peace I give is a gift the world cannot give. So, don't be troubled or afraid. Remember what I told you: I am going away, but I will come back to you again. If you really loved me, you would be happy that I am going to the Father, who is greater than I am. I have told you these things before they happen so that when they do happen, you will believe. ' don't have much more time to talk to you, because the ruler of this world approaches. He has no power over me, but I will do what the Father requires of me, so that the world will know that I love the Father. Come, let's be going."**

Apostle Paul continued the discussion as to peace in Romans 5:1-5 (NLT), which says, ***"Therefore, since we have been made right in God's sight by faith, we have peace with God because of what Jesus Christ our Lord has done for us. Because of our faith, Christ has brought us into this place of undeserved privilege where we now stand, and we confidently and joyfully look forward to sharing God's glory. We***

can rejoice, too, when we run into problems and trials, for we know that they help us develop endurance. And endurance develops strength of character, and character strengthens our confident hope of salvation. And this hope will not lead to disappointment. For we know how dearly God loves us, because he has given us the Holy Spirit to fill our hearts with his love."

SPIRITUAL GIFTS

You are unique and necessary to the body of Christ. We are each given spiritual gifts, including you! They may differ from each individual; however, they are each required to make up the community at large, one not less important than the other. Romans 12:3-8 (NLT) states, ***"Because of the privilege and authority God has given me, I give each of you this warning: Don't think you are better than you really are. Be honest in your evaluation of yourselves, measuring yourselves by the faith God has given us. Just as our bodies have many parts and each part has a special function, so it is with Christ's body. We are many parts of one body, and we all belong to each other. In his grace, God has given us different gifts for doing certain things well. So, if God has given you the ability to prophesy, speak out with as much faith as God has given you. If your gift is serving others, serve them well. If you are a teacher, teach well. If your gift is to encourage others, be encouraging. If it is giving, give generously. If God has given you leadership ability, take the responsibility seriously. And if you have a gift for showing kindness to others, do it gladly."***

Reverend Ronald Owens of Mount Olive A.M.E. sent emails to members of the church, which contained a list of spiritual gifts. The list was not all-inclusive, but it was vast. He was trying to encourage the participation of the church members. He wanted each one to see their value to the church by listing spiritual gifts that they may not have considered. Everyone could find at least one gift that they had been blessed with by God. It has been proven that helping others can provide a sense of purpose. The following is the modified list:

- Administration steers the body toward the accomplishment of God-given goals and directives by planning, organizing, and supervising others within the Church body.
- Discipleship provides leadership over the church body while maintaining authority over spiritual matters.
- Celibacy as a religious decision to voluntarily remain single without regret and with the ability to maintain controlled sexual impulses to serve the Lord without distraction.
- Discernment is the ability to clearly distinguish truth from error by judging whether the behavior or teaching is from God, Satan, human error, or human power.
- Evangelism is to be a messenger of the good news of the Gospel Outreach, sharing the Gospel.
- Exhortation provides someone with words of encouragement, comfort, consolation, and counsel to help them be all God wants from them.
- Faith is to be firmly persuaded of God's power and promises so his will can be accomplished according to his purpose. The

display of such a confidence in God and his Word, circumstances and obstacles do not shake that conviction.

- Giving is the willingness to share what material resources you have with liberality and cheerfulness without thought of return.
- Healing allows oneself to be used as a means through which God makes people whole physically, emotionally, mentally, or spiritually.
- Helps provide the support or assistance to others in the body, which allows them to be free to minister to others.
- Hospitality gives warm welcome upon people, even strangers, into one's home or church as a means of serving those in need of food or lodging.
- Knowledge is the ability to learn as much about the Bible as possible through the gathering of much information and the analyzing of that data.
- Leadership allows a person to stand before people in such a way as to attend to the direction of the body with such care and diligence to motivate others to get involved in the accomplishment of these goals.
- Martyrdom gives over one's life to suffer or to be put to death for the cause of Christ.
- Mercy is to be sensitive toward those who are suffering, whether physically, mentally, or emotionally, to feel genuine sympathy with their misery, speaking words of compassion

but more so caring for them with deeds of love to help alleviate their distress.

- Miracles allow for the performance of mighty deeds enabled by God which acknowledges its supernatural origin and means.
- Missionary is to minister to another who may not have heard the Good News Gospel through Outreach, Express love, and compassion.
- Pastoral, which makes one responsible for the spiritual growth, caring, protecting, guiding, and feeding a group of believers entrusted to one's care.
- Prophecy is to tell of future events as it pertains to God through the spirit.
- Service is the ability to both identify the needs of the body of the Church and the willingness to perform the tasks.
- Teaching is to instruct others on the Bible in a logical and systematic way to communicate the word of God, so that the believers will understand, believe, and grow.
- Speaking in tongues allows one to speak in a language not previously learned, so that unbelievers can hear God's message in their own language, or the body be edified.
- Interpretation of tongues translates the message of someone who has spoken in tongues.
- Voluntary poverty means to purposely live an impoverished lifestyle, lacking financially or materialistically, to serve and aid others with your material resources.

- Wisdom is the application of knowledge to life in such a way as to make spiritual truths quite relevant and practical in proper decision-making and daily life situations.

The Bible contains and discusses “personal and spiritual identity” in depth. The bottom line is that to chase anything other than God, including money, will leave you unfilled, unsatisfied and can lead to negative consequences. Whereas when you are one with God, not only are you blessed with various gifts, but you are a part of the body of Christ.

"OH, THE DEPTH OF THE RICHES BOTH OF THE WISDOM AND KNOWLEDGE OF GOD! HOW UNSEARCHABLE ARE HIS JUDGMENTS AND HIS WAYS PAST FIND OUT!"

Romans 11:33 (NKJV)

STEP ELEVEN

BLESSINGS FROM GOD

God has blessed us in ways that are known and unknown. But what is a Blessing? A "blessing" is defined as the act or words of a person who blesses, who conveys a special favor, mercy or benefit. To bless can also mean to invoke God's favor, approval, or good wishes upon a person. While "favor" is similar to blessing. It is defined as gaining approval, acceptance, special benefits, or blessings. The Lord is in accord with an individual and has shown gracious kindness towards them by showing them favor through the act of blessing them.

Have you heard the phrase, "Count Your Blessings?" Actually, it is impossible to count "all" of your blessings. On September 3, 2020, I facilitated a bible study, and we were studying Psalm 106:2 (NKJV). I asked a question to the group, what is meant by ***"Who can utter the mighty acts of the LORD? Who can declare all His praise?"*** The answers varied. Many of the participants believed that as Christians, we are the witnesses to the miraculous acts of God and Jesus Christ. The problem is that we were born two thousand years after Jesus Christ. Certainly, we are not able to provide an eyewitness account of those miracles he performed while in the body of man. A few of the answers referred to the book of Genesis where God created man. No one is in the position of stating the mighty acts of God. However, there was one participant who stated, ***"Oh, the depth of the riches both of the wisdom and knowledge of God! How unsearchable are His judgments and His ways past finding out!"*** Romans 11:33 (NKJV). It lets us know the blessings bestowed upon us by God are "unsearchable." This simply means that we are blessed in ways that are impossible to understand, because our blessings are both known and unknown.

Sometimes, when we are going through trials and tribulations, it is difficult to see our blessings clearly. On October 22, 2020, while I was preparing for bible study, I was seeking a humorous story, joke, antidote, etc., about thankfulness to end my bible study session. I went to atimetolaugh.com and told a few of the anecdotes that were listed, but as I told them, I realized it was easy to overlook the everyday blessings. Let me list a few for you and see if you agree.

I AM THANKFUL FOR the teenager who is not doing dishes but is watching T.V., because that means he is at home and not on the streets.

I AM THANKFUL FOR the clothes that fit a little too snug because it means I have enough to eat.

I AM THANKFUL FOR a lawn that needs mowing, windows that need cleaning, and gutters that need fixing, because it means I have a home.

I AM THANKFUL FOR the lady behind me in church that sings off key, because it means I can hear.

If you notice, the thankfulness statements are on things that we may never had considered, so we need to be open, to consider all blessings.

THE BEATITUDES

Jesus Christ began his first sermon, "The Sermon on the Mount" by listing nine blessings that are important to Christ. It contradicts our values. Our society values wealth, pride, popularity, and power. Jesus Christ showed true blessings are not related to the accumulation of things or powerful people, but of the characteristics that make a difference in someone else's life. The Sermon on the Mount began with the "Beatitudes," which means blessing or happy. Matthew 5:2-8 (ESV) says, "***And he opened his mouth and taught them, saying:***

> ***"Blessed are the poor in spirit, for theirs is the kingdom of heaven."***
>
> ***"Blessed are those who mourn, for they shall be comforted."***
>
> ***"Blessed are the meek, for they shall inherit the earth."***
>
> ***"Blessed are those who hunger and thirst for righteousness, for they shall be satisfied."***
>
> ***"Blessed are the merciful, for they shall receive mercy."***
>
> ***"Blessed are the pure in heart, for they shall see God."***
>
> ***"Blessed are the peacemakers, for they shall be called sons of God."***

"Blessed are those who are persecuted for righteousness' sake, for theirs is the kingdom of heaven."

"Blessed are you when others revile you and persecute you and utter all kinds of evil against you falsely on my account. Rejoice and be glad, for your reward is great in heaven, for so they persecuted the prophets who were before you."

BLESSINGS BASED ON THE ACT OF OBEDIENCE
THE OLD COVENANT

The first five books of the Old Testament are considered the Laws of Moses or the Torah. The last book of the Torah is Deuteronomy. It contains the farewell address of Moses. He formalized the Law or the Covenant between God and the Israelites who had been in the wilderness for almost forty years. The Israelites were close to the Promised Land however, Moses was to not take them any further. Joshua completed the mission.

Moses reminded the Israelites to honor the word of God. He said that they will be placed above all the nations of the earth if they obeyed his commandments. Continuing, he said the blessings would be so great as to overtake them. Of course, they must submit to the laws. They will be blessed with the fruit of God's true meaning, and their families will multiply. Their work, the herds, the young flock and their cities shall grow and prosper. Various methods shall defeat their enemies. All of their efforts will be successful. They will be landowners who will control their own destiny. Their spiritual blessings will come in abundance. And they would be established as Holy. So long as they love the Lord and obey his commandments.

In Deuteronomy 28:1-9 (ESV), Moses provided the Blessings for Obedience. It says, ***"And if you faithfully obey the voice of the LORD your God, being careful to do all his commandments that I command you today, the LORD your God will set you high above all the nations of the earth. And all these blessings shall come upon you and overtake you if you obey the voice of the LORD, your God. Blessed shall you be in the city and blessed shall you be in the field. Blessed shall be the fruit of your womb and the fruit of your ground and the fruit of your cattle, the increase of your herds and the young of your flock. Blessed shall be your basket and your kneading bowl. Blessed shall you be when you come in and blessed shall you be when you go out. 'The LORD will cause your enemies who rise against you to be defeated before you. They shall come out against you one way and flee before you seven ways. The LORD will command the blessing on you in your barns and in all that you undertake. And he will bless you in the land that the LORD your God is giving you. The LORD will establish you as a people holy to himself, as he has sworn to you, if you keep the commandments of the LORD your God and walk in his ways."***

BLESSINGS BASED ON THE ACT OF FAITH, NOT WORKS THE NEW COVENANT

Our greatest spiritual blessing is the gift of salvation, everlasting life. This is discussed in the New Testament as the New Covenant. It replaces the old covenants made with Moses and the Israelites. The New Covenant is found in Luke 22:17-20 (NKJV). It says, "***After taking the cup, he gave thanks and said, 'Take this and divide it among you. For I tell you I will not drink again from the fruit of the vine until the kingdom of God comes. And he took bread, gave thanks and broke it, and gave it to them, saying, 'This is my body given for you; do this in remembrance of me.' In the same way, after the supper he took the cup, saying, "This cup is the new covenant in my blood, which is poured out for you.***"

The New Testament opens with the four Gospels: Matthew, Mark, Luke, and Peter. Each of them talks about the birth, life, ministry, death, and resurrection of Jesus Christ. They are called "the Good News Doctrine or the Good News Gospels." The New Testament transforms the word of God and we can see the transfiguration of Jesus Christ within the Gospels. The significance is that Jesus Christ is the living sacrifice. He was born through God's divine intervention. He lived among men, teaching the word of God. He died on the cross for the sins of man, through which he offers salvation to those who have faith in him. He left a comforter, a counselor, the Holy Spirit to indwell within you, bringing you closer to God.

The requirements that were set forth in the Covenant with Moses have changed. They are no longer applicable. Apostle Paul in several of his writings said that in order to be saved with the blood of Jesus Christ, you must come through him in Faith, not by works. God's new covenant was not only for the Jews, but for the Gentiles, male and female, slave and freeborn, etc., which made it transformative. No one group was rejected. Galatians 3:25-29 (NKJV) says, "***Now that this faith has come, we are no longer under a guardian. So, in Christ Jesus you are all children of God through faith, for all of you who were baptized into Christ have clothed yourselves with Christ. There is neither Jew nor Gentile, neither slave nor free, nor is there male and female, for you are all one in Christ Jesus. If you belong to Christ, then you are Abraham's seed, and heirs according to the promise."***

Through his thirteen books, Apostle Paul, in the New Testament, tells us that we are blessed, that salvation is a gift to those who have faith. He stated in Romans 1:16-17, (ESV), "***For I am not ashamed of the gospel, for it is the power of God for salvation to everyone who believes, to the Jew first and also to the Greek. For in it the righteousness of God is revealed from faith for faith, as it is written, 'The righteous shall live by faith."*** In fact, he stated that salvation is not given due to "works" but by faith. His teaching is significant because it lets you know that salvation is through the faith or belief in Jesus Christ. You are not condemned if you cannot tithe or take part in one or more church groups. Nor are you required to say a Hail Mary or any other liturgy that is prescribed by church teaching and not the teaching of Jesus Christ. Nor does it say that we can continue to act as if we are part of this world. By accepting Jesus Christ, the Holy Spirit will help us grow in the Lord. Yet, the Bible reminds us that what you sow, you will reap.

In John 2:7-14 (ESV), it provides for "the New Commandment." It says, ***"Beloved, I am writing you no new commandment, but an old commandment that you had from the beginning. The old commandment is the word that you have heard. At the same time, it is a new commandment that I am writing to you, which is true in him and in you, because the darkness is passing away and the true light is already shining. Whoever says he is in the light and hates his brother is still in darkness. Whoever loves his brother abides in the light, and in him there is no cause for stumbling. But whoever hates his brother is in the darkness and walks in the darkness, and does not know where he is going, because the darkness has blinded his eyes."***

> ***"I am writing to you, little children,***
> ***because your sins are forgiven for his name's sake.***
> ***I am writing to you, fathers,***
> ***because you know him who is from the beginning.***
> ***I am writing to you, young men,***
> ***because you have overcome the evil one.***
> ***I write to you, children,***
> ***because you know the Father.***
> ***I write to you, fathers,***
> ***because you know him who is from the beginning.***
> ***I write to you, young men,***
> ***because you are strong,***
> ***and the word of God abides in you,***
> ***and you have overcome the evil one."***

We have been blessed in ways that we are unable to fathom. We have to continue to have faith that these blessings will continue in a way that will make our walk in this life easier.

"AND WE KNOW THAT ALL THINGS WORK TOGETHER FOR GOOD TO THOSE WHO LOVE GOD, TO THOSE WHO ARE THE CALLED ACCORDING TO HIS PURPOSE"

Romans 8:28 (NKJV)

STEP TWELVE
BE GRATEFUL

When we are grateful, thankful, and appreciative of what we are given, our outlook changes for the better. We woke up this morning. That is a reason to be grateful. We have eyes to see, ears to hear, and a mouth to speak. These are all reasons to be grateful. We have family and friends, reasons to be grateful. A new day, which represents a new beginning, reason to be grateful. And the fact that Jesus Christ died for our sins, sent a Helper, a Comforter, are reasons for us to be grateful.

I will admit it is hard to be grateful when you are not feeling good about your current life circumstances or you are uncertain about your future. But showing gratitude for the smallest of things has benefits seen and unseen. Being grateful has many benefits:

- Gratitude allows us to acknowledge our blessings.
- Gratitude causes our attitudes to change.
- Gratitude is a partner to both Faith and Hope.
- Gratitude acknowledges that God is present in our lives.

- Gratitude encourages the expansion of our spiritual blessings.
- Gratitude reflects appreciation not only to God, but to others.
- Gratitude encourages other people to want to reach out and help us.
- Gratitude is a component of wisdom.
- Gratitude can extend your longevity.
- Gratitude can increase your joy of living.
- Gratitude can attract others to us.
- Gratitude prepares us for additional blessings.

The Bible says that we should be grateful in all circumstances. 1 Thessalonians 5:18 (NIV) states, ***"Give thanks in all circumstances; for this is the will of God in Christ Jesus for you."*** Colossians 3:17 (NIV) states, ***"And whatever you do, in word or deed, do everything in the name of the Lord Jesus, giving thanks to God the Father through him."*** James 1:17 (NIV) *states,* ***"Every good gift and every perfect gift is from above, coming down from the Father of lights with whom there is no variation or shadow due to change."*** Psalm 107:1 (NIV) *states*, ***"Oh give thanks to the LORD, for he is good, for his steadfast love endures forever!"*** Romans 8:28 (NIV) states, ***"And we know that for those who love God all things work together for good, for those who are called according to his purpose."***

Sometimes, when I dwell on the negative or simply have bad thoughts, I have to say to myself, "the Devil is a liar," so those thoughts don't take over. The world can be unjust, unfair, and unsatisfying. It can be a violent and scary world. It can cause you to live in fear, be depressed and search for a way out. Now, we have an extra layer of concern with Covid-19. We must practice social distancing, so no hugs and kisses. We must wear a mask, no obvious smiles that can lighten the day. Therefore, we must use all the tools in our toolbox, which includes being thankful for that which is good, for that which keeps us moving-on and for that which keeps us growing and maturing.

My mother loves the book of Psalms. When she is asked or if she volunteers to read the Scripture as a part of the devotional team, she is always prepared with one of the Psalms that is encouraging. But there are several that speak to gratitude and thanksgiving. Let's look at Psalm 138:1-8 (ESV):

> ***"I give you thanks, O LORD, with my whole heart;***
> ***before the gods I sing your praise;***
> ***I bow down toward your holy temple***
> ***and give thanks to your name for your steadfast love and your faithfulness,***
> ***For you have exalted above all things***
> ***your name and your word.***
> ***On the day I called, you answered me;***
> ***my strength of soul you increased.***
> ***All the kings of the earth shall give you thanks, O LORD,***
> ***for they have heard the words of your mouth,***
> ***and they shall sing of the ways of the LORD,***
> ***for great is the glory of the LORD.***
> ***For though the LORD is high, he regards the lowly,***
> ***but the haughty he knows from afar.***
> ***Though I walk in the midst of trouble,***
> ***you preserve my life;***
> ***you stretch out your hand against the wrath of my enemies,***
> ***and your right hand delivers me.***
> ***The LORD will fulfill his purpose for me;***
> ***your steadfast love, O LORD, endures forever.***
> ***Do not forsake the work of your hands."***

This Psalmist gave thanks for God's steadfast love and faithfulness. He gave thanks to God for answering prayers. He gave thanks to God for considering the lowly. And he gave thanks to God for preserving his life, protecting him from the enemy, and fulfilling his purpose.

There is a story that I would like to share that demonstrates suffering, the miracle of healing, and the gift of gratitude. It is the story of the Ten Lepers as found in Luke 17:11-19 (ESV), it says, ***"On the way to Jerusalem he was passing along between Samaria and Galilee. And as he entered a village, he was met by ten lepers, who stood at a distance and lifted up their voices, saying, 'Jesus, Master, have mercy on us.' When he saw them, he said to them, 'Go and show yourselves to the priests.' And as they went, they were cleansed. Then one of them, when he saw that he was healed, turned back, praising God with a loud voice; and he fell on his face at Jesus' feet, giving him thanks. Now he was a Samaritan. Then Jesus answered, 'Were not ten cleansed? Where are the nine? Was no one found to return and give praise to God except this foreigner?' And he said to him, "Rise and go your way; your faith has made you well."***

The significance of the story of the Ten Lepers is that ten of the Lepers sought mercy as Jesus Christ passed through Samaria and Galilee. "Jesus saw them" is important because most people would have tried to stay as far as possible; overlooking them due to their condition, yet Jesus Christ saw them. He told the lepers to go to the Priest, pursuant to the thirteenth and fourteenth chapters of the book of Leviticus. As they were walking to the Priest, one noticed he was healed and came back to Jesus

Christ to thank and praise him. He was a mixed-race Samaritan, while the others were Jewish. The ones more likely to thank Jesus because of their background did not. The one who was least likely to understand the significance of what occurred to him, the non-Jewish stranger, returned to show his gratitude.

There is a similar story in 2 Kings 5. Just as in the story of the Ten Lepers, Naaman, the Gentile was also healed of leprosy. Both Naaman and the Samaritan leper were foreigners who sought healing from a Godly Jew. Both were ordered to perform a small, seemingly irrelevant action prior to the healing taking place. Elisha told Naaman to bathe in the river Jordan seven times. Jesus told the ten lepers to show themselves to the priest, who could certify a healing but who could not heal a leper. In both stories, healing took place only after they obeyed the man of God. Both Naaman and the Samaritan returned to praise God. Elisha's closing words to Naaman were, ***"Go in peace"*** 2 Kings 5:19 (ESV). Jesus' closing words to the Samaritan were, ***"And he said to him,*** **"Rise and go your way; your faith has made you well."** Luke 17:19 (ESV)

Gratitude and thankfulness are themes throughout the Bible. It is a characteristic that is valued by God and those who believe in him. Psalm 118 is a psalm of thanksgiving. It says to give thanks to the Lord for He is good, for His steadfast love endures forever. It gives many reasons to be thankful. Psalm 118:1:13 (ESV) says:

"Oh, give thanks to the LORD, for he is good;
for his steadfast love endures forever!

Let Israel say,
"His steadfast love endures forever."

Let the house of Aaron say,
"His steadfast love endures forever."
Let those who fear the LORD say,
"His steadfast love endures forever."

Out of my distress I called on the LORD;
the LORD answered me and set me free.
The LORD is on my side; I will not fear.
What can man do to me?
The LORD is on my side as my helper;
I shall look in triumph on those who hate me.

It is better to take refuge in the LORD
than to trust in man.
It is better to take refuge in the LORD
than to trust in princes.

All nations surrounded me;
in the name of the LORD I cut them off!
They surrounded me, surrounded me on every side;
in the name of the LORD I cut them off!
They surrounded me like bees;
they went out like a fire among thorns;
in the name of the LORD I cut them off!
I was pushed hard, so that I was falling,
but the LORD helped me."

THE STORY OF HANNAH

1 Samuel 1 tells a wonderful story about a woman named Hannah. She was very depressed because she desired a child, but she could not conceive. She prayed to God nonstop. Eventually, she bore a son. She showed her gratitude by giving the blessing, her son that she received through God's miracles, back to him. The story began by saying, ***"There***

was a man named Elkanah who lived in Ramah in the region of Zuphin the hill country of Ephraim . . . Elkanah had two wives, Hannah and Peninnah. Peninnah had children, but Hannah did not." 1 Samuel 1:1-2 (NLT)

The family would take an annual pilgrim to worship and to make a sacrifice. After the prayers, the meat would be shared between the various members of the family. "***Each year Elkanah would travel to Shiloh to worship and sacrifice to the LORD of Heaven's Armies at the Tabernacle. The priests of the LORD at that time were the two sons of Eli—Hophni and Phinehas. On the days Elkanah presented his sacrifice, he would give portions of the meat to Peninnah and each of her children. And though he loved Hannah, he would give her only one choice portion because the LORD had given her no children. So Peninnah would taunt Hannah and make fun of her because the LORD had kept her from having children."*** 1 Samuel 1:3-6 (NLT)

As each year came and went, Hannah would grow more depressed because she did not have a child. ***"Once after a sacrificial meal at Shiloh, Hannah got up and went to pray. Eli the priest was sitting at his customary place beside the entrance of the Tabernacle. Hannah was in deep anguish, crying bitterly as she prayed to the LORD. And she made this vow: 'O LORD of Heaven's Armies, if you will look upon my sorrow and answer my prayer and give me a son, then I will give him back to you. He will be yours for his entire lifetime, and as a sign that he has been dedicated to the LORD, his hair will never be cut."*** 1 Samuel 1:9-11 (NLT)

The Priest, Eli, believing she was drunk, questioned Hannah. ***"As she was praying to the LORD, Eli watched her. Seeing her lips moving but hearing no sound, he thought she had been drinking. 'Must you come here drunk?' he demanded. 'Throw away your wine!' 'Oh no, sir!' she replied. 'I haven't been drinking wine or anything stronger. But I am very discouraged, and I was pouring out my heart to the LORD. Don't think I am a wicked woman! For I have been praying out of great anguish and sorrow.' 'In that case,' Eli said, 'go in peace! May the God of Israel grant the request you have asked of him."*** 1 Samuel 1:12-17 (NLT)

Hannah was so grateful to the Lord for allowing her to have a son that she dedicated him as a servant of the Lord. ***"And she said, 'Oh, my lord! As you live, my lord, I am the woman who was standing here in your presence, praying to the LORD. For this child I prayed, and the LORD has granted me my petition that I made to him. Therefore, I have lent him to the LORD. As long as he lives, he is lent to the LORD."*** 1 Samuel 1:26-28 (NLT)

The story of Hannah reminds us that the blessings that we desire may not come when we want them. It also shows that we may already be blessed, but don't recognize the blessing. In the case of Hannah, her husband loved her so much that he gave her a double portion. When God blessed her, she demonstrated her gratitude. Therefore, we, too, must be grateful for our blessings, both known and unknown.

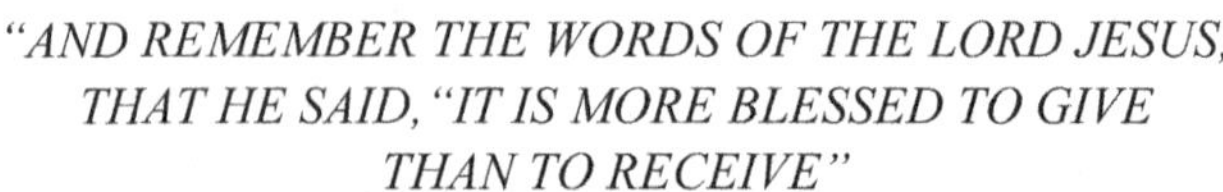

"AND REMEMBER THE WORDS OF THE LORD JESUS, THAT HE SAID, "IT IS MORE BLESSED TO GIVE THAN TO RECEIVE"

Acts 20:35 (NKJV)

STEP THIRTEEN

INTERCESSION – HELPING OTHERS

The concept of intercession is the act of intervening on behalf of another. While intercessory prayer is the act of praying on behalf of someone else. Intercession follows the mission of Jesus Christ. Of the commandments, Jesus Christ said that the greatest commandment is to love the Lord with all your heart, soul and mind and love your neighbor as yourself. Matthew 22:36-40 (NLT) says the following: ***"Teacher, which is the most important commandment in the law of Moses?" Jesus replied, 'You must love the LORD your God with all your heart, all your soul, and all your mind.' This is the first and greatest commandment. A second is equally important: 'Love your neighbor as yourself.' The entire law and all the demands of the prophets are based on these two commandments."***

Years ago, my niece, my brother's daughter, came to live with me. We were both having trouble adjusting to the changes that were taking place. I suggested we go to a local women's shelter to volunteer. I hoped that by working with others, we could see that there were people worse off than we were, that we could have a sense of purpose, and that we would be encouraged to set personal goals that could be of benefit to our community and not just limited to ourselves.

I have worked with people for years, whether I was a volunteer mediating conflicts through my legal practice; counseling individuals into the right mortgage product for them or if I was encouraging and motivating someone who was down on their luck. It has given me a sense of purpose when I am told that my actions have made a difference in someone's life.

An article in Psychology Today called, "In Helping Others, You Help Yourself," which was published on May 30, 2018, the author, Marianna Pogosyan, stated, "Research has found many examples of how doing good, in ways big or small, not only *feels* good but also *does* us good. For instance, the well-being-boosting and depression-lowering benefits of volunteering have been repeatedly documented. As has the sense of meaning and purpose that often accompanies altruistic behavior. Even when it comes to money, spending it on others predicts an increase in happiness compared to spending it on ourselves. Moreover, there is now neural evidence from fMRI studies suggesting a link between generosity and happiness in the brain. For example, donating money to charitable organizations activates the same (mesolimbic) regions of the brain that respond to monetary rewards or sex. In fact, the mere intent and commitment to generosity can stimulate neural change and make people happier."

On December 15, 2018, Stephanie Booth wrote an article in Healthline called, "How Helping Others Affect Your Brain." During a recent study, researchers at the University of Pittsburgh gave 45 volunteers an option: They could complete a task that benefited themselves, a charity, or a particular friend in need. Afterwards, a brain scan showed a noticeable — and fascinating — difference based on their choice. Not only did the participants who helped others display increased activity in two "reward centers" of their brain, but they had *decreased* activity in three other regions that help inform the body's physical response to stress through lower blood pressure and reduced inflammation.

A second study from the University of Pittsburgh, this time utilizing nearly 400 volunteers who were asked to self-report their "giving" habits, showed similar results. "Humans are born especially vulnerable and dependent on others," explained Tristen Inagaki, PhD, an assistant professor of psychology at the University of Pittsburgh who led both studies. "As a result, we require a prolonged period of intense caregiving following birth in order to survive." That instinctive desire to help others may depend on those specific areas of the brain. They guarantee more supportive behavior. "The same mechanisms that ensure giving to others may also contribute to the long-term health effects we see from giving," said Inagaki.

And there are plenty of other benefits. People who volunteer get sick less often and for shorter periods of time. In fact, they may go for longer periods without getting sick. They have also shown helping to improve a person's self-esteem, foster a rosier view of the world, decrease risky or problematic behaviors, and stave off depression can be effected by helping others. Plus, the more you help others, the more you *want* to keep helping.

BENEFITS OF HELPING ONE ANOTHER

Not only is it our responsibility to love another, but we should help one another. We are tied to our community whether we like it or not. Not just our physical community but our Christian community. The Bible has discussed intercession and loving one another. Let's consider what Philippians 2:1-4 (NLT) says, ***"Is there any encouragement from belonging to Christ? Any comfort from his love? Any fellowship together in the Spirit? Are your hearts tender and compassionate? Then make me truly happy by agreeing wholeheartedly with each other, loving one another, and working together with one mind and purpose. Don't be selfish; don't try to impress others. Be humble, thinking of others as better than yourselves. Don't look out only for your own interests, but take an interest in others, too."*** This verse tells us that to fulfill the joy of Jesus Christ requires us to be like-minded and humble, considering the interest of the other person.

It also makes a request of each of us. If the word of God encourages us, we should encourage others. If we receive comfort from his love, we should offer comfort to someone. It does not necessarily mean bringing someone into your home, but to reach out to who you can by word or deed. The Spirit of Christ should inspire us to think of others. Therefore, getting out of our own head and our own problems is essential if we are going to grow.

The Apostle Paul reminds us in Romans 15:1-4 (NLT) to assist one another. He said, ***"We who are strong must be considerate of those who are sensitive about things like this. We must not just please ourselves. We should help others do what is right and build them up in the Lord. For even Christ didn't live to please himself. As the Scriptures say, 'The insults of those who insult you, O God, have fallen on me.' Such things were written in the Scriptures long ago to teach us. And the Scriptures give us hope and encouragement as we wait patiently for God's promises to be fulfilled."*** When a person is in need, if he is in a weakened state, we should build them up. This can be done through prayer, through encouragement and or through specific action!

THE PARABLE OF THE GOOD SAMARITAN

The book of Luke gives an account of the story of the Good Samaritan. The backdrop of the story is that a man who is considered unclean, a mixed breed, not a Jew, from a place called "Samaria." This man steps in to help a stranger. However, he was not the first to see the man in need. Other men, a priest, a society nobleman, also saw the man in need, but they did nothing. This story repeats the greatest commandment.

It begins when a religious expert questions Jesus Christ. He wants Jesus to provide a definition as to who is a "neighbor." At first glance, the question appears harmless, however, he is attempting to entrap Jesus. Luke

10:25-20 (NLT) says, ***"One day an expert in religious law stood up to test Jesus by asking him this question:***

> ***"Teacher, what should I do to inherit eternal life?" Jesus replied, "What does the law of Moses say? How do you read it?" The man answered, "'You must love the LORD your God with all your heart, all your soul, all your strength, and all your mind.' And, 'Love your neighbor as yourself.' "Right!" Jesus told him. "Do this and you will live!" The man wanted to justify his actions, so he asked Jesus, "And who is my neighbor?"***

Instead of answering the question directly, Jesus put forth a parable to the expert. A riddle or analogy that would allow the expert to come to his own conclusion by answering the question himself.

> ***"Jesus replied with a story: 'A Jewish man was traveling from Jerusalem down to Jericho, and he was attacked by bandits. They stripped him of his clothes, beat him up, and left him half dead beside the road. 'By chance, a priest came along. But when he saw the man lying there, he crossed to the other side of the road and passed him by. A Temple assistant walked over and looked at him lying there, but he also passed by on the other side. 'Then a***

> ***despised Samaritan came along, and when he saw the man, he felt compassion for him. Going over to him, the Samaritan soothed his wounds with olive oil and wine and bandaged them. Then he put the man on his own donkey and took him to an inn, where he took care of him. The next day he handed the innkeeper two silver coins, telling him, 'Take care of this man. If his bill runs higher than this, I'll pay you the next time I'm here.' 'Now, which of these three would you say was a neighbor to the man who was attacked by bandits?" Jesus asked. The man replied, "The one who showed him mercy." Then Jesus said, "Yes, now go and do the same."*** Luke 10:30-37 (NLT)

The story of the Good Samaritan reminds us that we are connected to one another if you believe in Jesus Christ. Ephesians 2:19 reminds us that we are no longer strangers or foreigners in a strange land, that we are all part of the body of Christ. ***"Now, therefore, you are no longer strangers and foreigners, but fellow citizens with the saints and members of the household of God."***

There are many places within the Bible where we can see intercessory prayer at work. All we have to do is read the book of Psalms. Even the book of Exodus discusses intercessory prayer. There were several occasions that Moses prayed for the Israelite people. Moses asked God to forgive them when they were disobedient and impatient. ***"And he said, "If now I have found favor in your sight, O Lord, please let the Lord go***

in the midst of us, for it is a stiff-necked people, and pardon our iniquity and our sin, and take us for your inheritance." Exodus 34:9 (ESV)

While on the cross, dying for our sins, Jesus Christ prayed for those who were crucifying him. In Luke 23:34 (NKJV), it says, ***"Then Jesus said, "Father, forgive them, for they do not know what they do."*** Can you imagine being murdered and praying for your murderer?

Apostle Paul tells us to help the weak and remember the words of Jesus Christ in Acts 20:35 (ESV), it says, ***"In all things I have shown you that by working hard in this way we must help the weak and remember the words of the Lord Jesus, how he himself said, 'It is more blessed to give than to receive."***

When I was young, I would hear the phrase, it is better to give than receive. But as a child, you can only comprehend receiving and how it feels on Christmas morning when you look under the tree for presents or on your birthday. It is hard to believe that you would mature in a way that allows you to understand that in order for you to give, you must be blessed to give. For example, in order to give a present, more often than not, you must have the money to buy the present; the extra, the over and beyond your basic necessities. It is a blessing.

Being an intercessor, your focus changes from you to someone else. In order to get outside of your own head and allow time to heal; you must give of your time, energy, and love to someone else. It will make both a physical and emotion difference in your life. And it will be a benefit to your community at large.

"WRITE THE VISION AND MAKE IT PLAIN ON TABLETS, THAT HE MAY RUN WHO READS IT"

Habakkuk 2:2 (NKJV)

STEP FOURTEEN

NOT REALLY A STEP, REMEMBER TO WRITE IT DOWN

Write down your dreams, goals, and desires! Put it in a place where you can see it every day. It will help you to stay on task. In fact, write down the tasks that will help you accomplish your goals, too. Check off those tasks from your list as you complete each one. I know you heard this before, but this is the time to do it.

There are many benefits of writing things down:

First, it is an excellent way to express yourself, to state your fears or desires in a private setting.

Second, it allows you to get things off your chest, protecting you from unnecessary or unwanted confrontations.

Third, it is a way to provide affirmations to yourself.

Fourth, it helps you remember tasks and chores.

Fifth, it assists you with strategizing and planning.

Sixth, it memorializes events and/or activities.

Seventh, it can verify or confirm actions taken in the past.

Eighth, it is a great way to communicate.

Ninth, you can express your feelings or thoughts toward someone else.

Tenth, it can help you accomplish your goals. I am sure there are many other reasons for writing things down, too.

Sometimes, not often, when I am driving, walking the dog or just relaxing, a thought comes to mind, a great thought! Something that would alter the course of my life, something so great that I don't need to write it down because it is so life shattering that I would never forget it. But I forget it. Yes, it turns out that my thoughts really weren't life shattering, life altering nor great, but it could have changed my perspective, my attitude or influenced my strategy, if I only wrote it down. Now, I have learned to write things down or put it in my phone. I have reached the age where a "senior moment" is real. Writing ideas and thoughts is necessary.

Years ago, when I was separating from my husband, or should I say when my husband was separating from me, I went through a really dark spell. I was very depressed. I wrote notes to myself and placed them in the bathroom, in my car, or in my wallet. Some notes I cannot repeat because I am changed, okay not changed, but older. Some notes I can share. I would write "You are Beautiful!" "You are smart!" You are smarter than he is!" "Make things happen!" "You are a winner!" Each one would end with an exclamation mark. I would not believe the notes, however, they cheered me up anyway. Over time, I felt more like myself, affirmed.

Writing things down is not new. In fact, there are many places in the Bible where some individuals were told to write some things down. In Exodus:17, Moses was told to write down the defeat of Amalek, so it would be memorialized forever. Memorialized simply means to create something that causes people to remember a person, thing, or event. I am not sure who the Amalek people are, but I know they were defeated because it was written down. Exodus 17:14-16 (NKJV) says, ***"Then the LORD said to Moses, 'Write this as a memorial in a book and recite it in the ears of Joshua, that I will utterly blot out the memory of Amalek from under heaven."***

There were several other times in which God told someone to write it down. Again, the Lord told Moses to get two stone tablets and that he would write the words, not Moses. In Exodus 34:1(ESV), the LORD said to Moses, ***"Cut for yourself two tablets of stone like the first, and I will write on the tablets the words that were on the first tablets, which you broke."*** And God repeated the request in Exodus 34:27-28 (ESV), the Lord told Moses to write it down, himself. He said, ***"And the LORD said to Moses, "Write these words, for in accordance with these words I have made a covenant with you and with Israel." So. he was there with the LORD forty days and forty nights. He neither ate bread nor drank water. And he wrote on the tablets the words of the covenant, the Ten Commandments."***

Habakkuk is a minor Prophet who was so frustrated with what he saw around him he questioned God. In Habakkuk 1:1 (ESV), the Prophet cried, ***"Oh Lord, How Long Should I cry for Help?"*** When I saw this story in the Bible, I could not believe it. I felt alone, surrounded by injustice, hollering to the Lord, "Oh Lord, How Long?" I did not realize that this question had been asked and answered a thousand times.

But in the Prophet Habakkuk's case, God answered him personally. He began by telling the Prophet Habakkuk to write his answer down. God wanted it known that the opposition, his adversary, was greedy like death, never having enough, trying to collect nations for himself, his own people. In Habakkuk 2:2-3 (ESV), the Lord answered:

> ***"Write the vision;***
> ***make it plain on tablets,***
> ***so he may run who reads it.***
> ***For still the vision awaits its appointed time;***
> ***it hastens to the end—it will not lie.***
> ***If it seems slow, wait for it.***
> ***it will surely come; it will not delay."***

The Prophet Jeremiah was told to write it down, too. In fact, the Lord wanted Jeremiah to write a book and make sure it contained all the words that he had spoken to Jeremiah. Because the Lord had tried various means of getting the Israelites' attention, but to no avail. In Jeremiah, 30:2-3 (ESV), it reads, ***"The word that came to Jeremiah from the LORD: "Thus says the LORD, the God of Israel: Write in a book all the words that I have spoken to you. For behold, days are coming, declares the LORD, when I will restore the fortunes of my people, Israel and Judah, says the LORD, and I will bring them back to the land that I gave to their fathers, and they shall take possession of it."*** The Lord wanted it written that his people will be brought back whole, given the land of their fathers. This was after they were to be punished for their disobedience.

The book of Revelation is the last book of the bible. John the Elder wrote it while on the island of Patmos. This book is considered both apocalyptic and prophetic. John saw visions which included a battle between Satan and his minions, as well as Jesus and the angels of heaven. He was commanded by the Lord to write what he saw in Revelation 1:10-11 (ESV), which says, ***"I was in the Spirit on the Lord's day, and I heard behind me a loud voice like a trumpet saying, 'Write what you see in a book and send it to the seven churches, to Ephesus and to Smyrna and to Pergamum and to Thyatira and to Sardis and to Philadelphia and to Laodicea."*** Further down in Revelations 1:19 (ESV), there is another demand to write it down. It says, **"Write therefore the things that you have seen, those that are and those that are to take place after this."**

Even in the Gospels or "Good News Doctrine", the first four books of the New Testament which teach about the origins, birth, ministry, death, resurrection, and ascension of Jesus Christ. They are noted for their eyewitness accounts of the life of Jesus Christ. One of the writers of the Gospel is the Apostle Luke. Luke is the only Gentile, non-Jewish individual to pen a book or books in the Bible. He was a physician. In his prologue, he said his goal was to provide an ordered account of the events of Jesus' life through a written history. Luke 1:1-4 (ESV) says,

> ***"Inasmuch as many have undertaken to compile a narrative of the things that have been accomplished among us, just as those who from the beginning were eyewitnesses and ministers of the word have delivered them to us, it seemed good to me also, having followed all things closely for some time past, to write an orderly account for***

you, most excellent Theophilus, that you may have certainty concerning the things you have been taught."

Therefore, keep your pen and paper, tablet or phone nearby. And write your goals, affirmations, and everyday thoughts. Before you know it, you will no longer be starting, but in motion.

"WRITE THE VISION AND MAKE IT PLAIN ON TABLETS, THAT HE MAY RUN WHO READS IT"

Habakkuk 2:2 (NKJV)

STEP FIFTEEN
STAY ENCOURAGED; IT CAN BE HARD!

Being encouraged is a state of mind that is affected by our circumstances. It is hard to be hopeful, confident or to feel supported when you feel alone, lost, or empty. Even when friends and family try to lift you up with kind words or deeds. You probably heard something like, *"I know things are difficult right now, but I also know you've got what it takes to get through it."* *"I'm so sorry you're going through this, but this too shall pass."* Or "*You're doing exactly what you should be doing. Hang in there."* Have you ever wondered; how do they know I got what it takes to get through it? How do they know it will pass? It feels like forever. Or how do they know I am doing exactly what I should be doing? Can they see what I am doing? Do they know that I am sleeping all day, refusing to get out of bed? Yet, I have made similar statements in the hopes of encouraging someone else.

The word courageous comes out of the word encouraged. Yet, the meanings of these words are different. To be courageous is to be bold, strong, and intent. While encourage means to be hopeful, confident and to feel supported. To survive through the bad times, both hopefulness and the intent to be strong must be present. Our own feelings can hamper or prevent us from being encouraged.

Did you know that your perception of reality can be affected by your own feelings? When you feel good, the world seems like a nicer place. When you feel bad, you are asking yourself when will the tribulation take place, can't God see the violence and injustice? Our feelings affect our outlook, our ability to be encouraged and our mood. We have to learn how to control our feelings.

Several years ago, I went on a cruise with my youngest nephew. We had a wonderful time. I have pictures to prove it! We were on the Oasis of the Seas, one of the largest ships at that time. He was just twenty years old. He met a group of kids on the ship that he hung out with. He won the volleyball trophy. He went from one end of the ship to the next. I thought he had the time of his life. Yet, I knew he was eager to see his girlfriend, Kathryn. The ship docked as scheduled, and we were scheduled to fly out of Fort Lauderdale to BWI later that evening. I rented a car so we could see some of the sights before returning home. My nephew fell asleep while I drove. When he awoke, he thought we missed our flight. He became angry and obnoxious. In fact, he insulted me and then said that I was in my feelings. Can you imagine taking your child on a trip only to be insulted by him? But his statement was an accurate representation of how I felt. *"I was in my feelings."* For a moment. I would not let him steal my joy. But that was a decision I had to make.

When I was growing up, we did not use the term "*in your feelings*." However, feelings can control your outlook. I learned some time ago that I am the only one that can control my feelings. I can choose how long I want to remain angry or if I am angry at all. My responses to the outside world are mind to make. It was necessary to be aware of how you are feeling and control those feelings because they control your thoughts and behavior. When I was young, I was quick to respond, in a hurry to act out. But as I have gotten older, I realize it is a wise man that strategize their next steps. In fact, Proverbs 25:28 (ESV) says, ***"A man without self-control is like a city broken into and left without walls."*** The imagery of Proverbs 25:28 should act as a warning that the cost of losing control can be great. We can lose our sense of stability, security, or safety. Being encouraged is a decision that you must make. You cannot wait until you are in the right mood or mindset. Your decision will control your mindset. Your mindset will control your behavior.

GIDEON

I would like to discuss the story of Gideon, which is found in the book of Judges. The backdrop of the story is that the Midianites had oppressed the Israelites for seven years. God allowed the oppression because of their disobedience. But it was about to change. Gideon, an Israelite, was working in the vinepress, threshing wheat so the Midianites would not see him. The Angel of God approaches Gideon and calls him, "O Mighty Man of Valor." When Gideon hears these words, he questions the Angel. He does not feel like a "Mighty Warrior." He feels oppressed. ***And Gideon said to him, "Please, my lord, if the LORD is with us, why then has all this happened to us? And where are all his wonderful***

deeds that our fathers recounted to us, saying, 'Did not the LORD bring us up from Egypt?' But now the LORD has forsaken us and given us into the hand of Midian." Judges 6:13 (ESV)

But the Angel of God is speaking to not what Gideon is but what he will become. He has been tasked with saying the Israelites from the Midianites. ***"And the LORD turned to him and said, "Go in this might of yours and save Israel from the hand of Midian; do not I send you?"*** Judges 6:14 (ESV)

Gideon was not courageous, nor was he encouraged. He viewed his tribe as weak and himself as small. His behavior followed that view. ***"Please, Lord, how can I save Israel? Behold, my clan is the weakest in Manasseh, and I am the least in my father's house." And the LORD said to him, "But I will be with you, and you shall strike the Midianites as one man."*** Judges 6:15 (ESV)

Even after God promised he would remain with Gideon, he still demanded a sign from God. ***"And he said to him, "If now I have found favor in your eyes, then show me a sign that it is you who speak with me."***

The first assignment God gave Gideon was to pull down the altars of the false gods, Baal and Asherah. However, he was too afraid to do it during the day, so he did it at night. "***So Gideon took ten men of his servants and did as the LORD had told him. But because he was too afraid of his family and the men of the town to do it by day, he did it by night."*** Judges 6:27 (ESV)

Due to fear and his lack of courage, Gideon asks for a second sign from God. ***"If you will save Israel by my hand, as you have said, behold, I am laying a fleece of wool on the threshing floor. If there is dew on the fleece alone, and it is dry on all the ground, then I shall know that you will save Israel by my hand, as you have said."*** Judges 6:36-37 (ESV)

God told Gideon to arise and go down against the camp of his enemies, for he would give them into his hand. But Gideon, being afraid, still needed reassurances and proof. So, God tells him to go with his servant, Purah, down to the camp and listen to what the men were saying, then he should be strengthened. Judges 7:13-14 (ESV) states, ***"When Gideon came, behold, a man was telling a dream to his comrade. And he said, "Behold, I dreamed a dream, and behold, a cake of barley bread tumbled into the camp of Midian and came to the tent and struck it so that it fell and turned it upside down, so that the tent lay flat." And his comrade answered, "This is no other than the sword of Gideon, the son of Joash, a man of Israel; God has given into his hand Midian and all the camp."***

It was only after hearing the words from his enemies did Gideon believe God. "As ***soon as Gideon heard the telling of the dream and its interpretation, he worshiped. And he returned to the camp of Israel and said, "Arise, for the Lord has given the host of Midian into your hand."*** Judge 7:15 (ESV)

Later, Gideon defeated the Midianites. But it was only after Gideon could get out of his own head or out of his feelings of discouragement and defeat.

Judges 8:22-23 (ESV) stood as a reminder that the Lord will rule over his people, not man. It says, ***"Then the men of Israel said to Gideon, "Rule over us, you and your son and your grandson also, for you have saved us from the hand of Midian." Gideon said to them, "I will not rule over you, and my son will not rule over you; the LORD will rule over you."***

Be encouraged, your hope comes from God!

ENCOURAGEMENT

While counseling individuals and couples, I have come to understand the need for encouragement. It offers hope during the time that may seem the darkest or bleak. It provides much needed reassurance. There is a tendency for people to feel alone or separated from the world when they are going through a crisis. It has the power to change an attitude or outlook. It can give a person the power to confront an issue that may appear to be overwhelming. It is said that we have entered the age of a global society, yet many people are afraid and by themselves, especially during this pandemic. Encouragement can be the nemesis to fear. Hope, Faith, and Peace can be the benefactors of encouragement. We all need to be encouraged and affirmed.

Have you ever considered the definition of "encouraged?" The Merriam-Webster dictionary says it means to inspire with courage, spirit, or hope. It also says it means to attempt to persuade. When you are feeling down-and-out, it is hard to inspire with courage, spirit or hope, but it is not impossible. In fact, we must be encouraged if we are to have a satisfying and fulfilled life. When you are discouraged, turn to the Bible because it is filled with encouraging and uplifting stories, poetry, and verses. In fact, several letters in the Bible are written for the purpose of encouraging the reader.

The Apostle Paul wrote thirteen books of the New Testament, including the book of Philippians. This book was written while the Apostle Paul was in prison. Although this book was written while he was in prison, it is one of the happiest books in the Bible. This book consists of several letters written to the Church of Philippi. It is meant to encourage the Church. He wanted to remind them that salvation comes through the son of God, Jesus Christ, who died on the cross and was resurrected three days later, redeeming their sins, and through faith in Jesus Christ, they would have everlasting life.

The Apostle Paul told the Church to guard their hearts and minds in Jesus Christ. Also, he reminded them not to be anxious about anything, but let their request be made known to God. This is advice we all should take to quiet our thoughts. In Philippians 4:4-9 (ESV), it says, "***Rejoice in the Lord always; again, I will say, Rejoice. Let your reasonableness be known to everyone. The Lord is at hand; do not be anxious about anything, but in everything by prayer and supplication with thanksgiving let your requests be made known to God. And the peace of God, which surpasses all understanding, will guard your hearts and your minds in Christ Jesus. Finally, brothers, whatever is true, whatever is honorable, whatever is just, whatever is pure, whatever is lovely, whatever is commendable, if there is any excellence, if there is anything***

worthy of praise, think about these things. What you have learned and received and heard and seen in me—practice these things, and the God of peace will be with you."

The Apostle Paul was in prison writing, ***"Rejoice." "Let Everyone see Christ in you." "Do not be anxious but Pray to the Lord."*** He even made an argument about the benefits of gratitude. He said to ***"practice these things that you have learned, received and heard."*** He also made it known that Christ is ***"honorable," "just," "pure," "lovely," and "true."*** Aren't his words encouraging? Yet, his circumstances were not.

The Apostle Paul also wrote the book of Colossians. It too is a prison epistle and consists of letters to the church of Colossae. It was a small, struggling church that was questioning his teachings. He told the church to remain together in Christ with the full assurance of God's mystery, which may be revealed through wisdom and knowledge. He let the church to know that he was with them in Spirit. He said these things to encourage the church to keep the faith. In Colossians 2:1-5 (ESV), he said, ***"For I want you to know how great a struggle I have for you and for those at Laodicea and for all who have not seen me face to face, that their hearts may be encouraged, being knit together in love, to reach all the riches of full assurance of understanding and the knowledge of God's mystery, which is Christ, in whom are hidden all the treasures of wisdom and knowledge. I say this in order that no one may delude you with plausible arguments. For though I am absent in body, yet I am with you in spirit, rejoicing to see your good order and the firmness of your faith in Christ."***

The Apostle Peter was one of the twelve disciples of Jesus Christ. In fact, Peter was one of the first of the disciples to acknowledge that Jesus was the Messiah to which Jesus said that he was the rock on which his church will be built. Peter denied Christ three times as prophesied by Jesus, but was forgiven. After the death of Christ, Peter, through the indwelling of the Holy Spirit, found his voice. He became a passionate speaker. He wrote two letters. In the second, he said to be aware of false teachers and prophets, there will be a punishment for those led astray. However, he also made an encouraging statement that I would like to include here. He said that one day for God is like a thousand years for man. He further said that God is giving us as much time as possible to repent or turn to him. It is not his slowness, but his patience that matters. 2 Peter 3:8-10 (ESV) says:

> ***"But do not overlook this one fact, beloved, that with the Lord one day is as a thousand years, and a thousand years as one day. The Lord is not slow to fulfill his promise as some count slowness, but is patient toward you, not wishing that any should perish, but that all should reach repentance. But the day of the Lord will come like a thief, and then the heavens will pass away with a roar, and the heavenly bodies will be burned up and dissolved, and the earth and the works that are done on it will be exposed."***

The Apostle Paul became a mentor to a young minister by the name of Timothy. He wrote letters of direction and encouragement to him by stating that the letter is a reminder of the commandments of the Lord and the predictions, including the fact that people will say where is your God, yet nothing has changed since creation. He told Timothy that those who desire to live a godly life will be persecuted. So, expect that bad things will happen, but God will right all wrongs for his people. 2 Timothy 3:12-16 (ESV) states the following, "***Indeed, all who desire to live a godly life in Christ Jesus will be persecuted, while evil people and impostors will go on from bad to worse, deceiving and being deceived. But as for you, continue in what you have learned and have firmly believed, knowing from whom you learned it and how from childhood you have been acquainted with the sacred writings, which are able to make you wise for salvation through faith in Christ Jesus. All Scripture is breathed out by God and profitable for teaching, for reproof, for correction, and for training in righteousness, that the man of God may be complete, equipped for every good work.***"

Many people think of King David as the writer of Psalms, but he did not write all of them. Keep in mind that the Psalms are prayers, songs, and poetry. The Law of Moses, again, the first five books of the Old Testament. Also called the Torah by the Hebrews. Or the Pentateuch by the Greeks. They attributed these writings to Moses. But it is believed that Moses wrote Psalms 91, too. It speaks to God's protection and refuge from danger. It is said that while Moses was completing the building of the Tabernacle in the desert; he wrote this Psalm. He had experienced many trials and tribulations with the Israelite people. Many who refused to obey the word of God. He needed encouragement. Psalms 91 (NKJV) is absolutely beautiful because it provides hope to the hopeless and encouragement to those who are discouraged. It lets you know God is your protector, your shield, and your refuge. Psalms 91:1-8 (NKJV) says:

"He who dwells in the secret place of the Most High
Shall abide under the shadow of the Almighty.
I will say of the LORD, 'He is my refuge and my fortress;
My God, in Him I will trust.'

Surely, he shall deliver you from the snare of the fowler
And from the perilous pestilence.
He shall cover you with His feathers,
And under His wings you shall take refuge;
His truth shall be your shield and buckler.
You shall not be afraid of the terror by night,
Nor of the arrow that flies by day,
Nor of the pestilence that walks in darkness,
Nor of the destruction that lays waste at noonday.

A thousand may fall at your side,
And ten thousand at your right hand;
But it shall not come near you.
Only with your eyes shall you look,
And see the reward of the wicked."

Stay Encouraged and seek God's refuge!

"I WILL SAY OF THE LORD, HE IS MY REFUGE AND MY FORTRESS; MY GOD, IN HIM I WILL TRUST"

Psalm 91:2 (NKJV)

STEP SIXTEEN

BE PERSISTENT!

At this point in your life, you may wonder how many times is necessary to continue to try. Well, the answer is different for each of us, yet it is the same. As long as you are alive, each day brings forth a new opportunity, a new adventure, and a new beginning. In Matthew 18:21-22, the Apostle Peter asked Jesus Christ, ***"Lord, how open shall my brother sin against me, and I forgive him? Up to seven times? Jesus said to him, I do not say to you, up to seven times, but up to seventy times seven."*** When faced with the question of how many times should we get up and try again, it is assumed that it should be at least seventy times seven.

Today follows yesterday. An old day with all of its baggage, including the failures, disappointments, and criticisms. Despite what happened yesterday, start today with a new positive attitude. Kick yesterday to the curb. You can't change what happened. There is no such thing as a "re-do" day. So, before you begin this day, remind yourself that you do not walk alone. Do not underestimate the fact that God walks with you. This should give you confidence that your efforts are worthwhile. Let go of whatever occurred yesterday, the day before that day and the days before that one. Learn from them. Grow wiser. But shake it off! Let it go. Galatians 6:9 (ESV) states, ***"And let us not grow weary of doing good, for in due season we will reap, if we do not give up."*** You do not have the luxury to give up!

To be persistent is to keep on getting up. There are benefits of being persistent. The chances of reaching your goal becomes greater. It allows you to think outside of the box. It will test the creativity within you for endurance and strength. Your knowledge and ability will expand into greater endeavors. The ability to take more chances with different outcomes will cause you to diversify. Your destiny is not in anyone else's hand, it is in your own. James_1:12 (ESV) states, ***"Blessed is the man who remains steadfast under trial, for when he has stood the test he will receive the crown of life, which God has promised to those who love him."***

Back in February 2017, Senator Elizabeth Warren was silenced at the confirmation of Alabama Senator Jeffrey Sessions, for the position of the Attorney General for the United States. Republican Majority Senate Leader, Mitch McConnell, said that Senator Elizabeth Warren had violated a senate rule. The slogan that came from this incident is "Nevertheless, She Persisted!" It became a rallying cry. Persistence means to continue firmly or obstinately in a course of action despite difficulty or opposition. Yes, we must continue in spite of opposition.

There have been periods in my life when I would tell my Aunt Mae that it was better to be a failure than a quitter. In order to have failed, you would have had to make an effort, make an attempt towards a goal. While quitting takes little or no effort at all. Sometimes, it is difficult to be persistent. However, if we are going to be successful, we must persist!

Jesus Christ told his Disciples the Parable of the Unjust Judge. The underlying story is that the women in the parable persisted. The story is about a widow who came before an unjust and unfair Judge. He did not care about her or her circumstances. He denied her request, not thinking any more about the widow. But she was persistent. She continued to come before the Judge making the same request. He finally tired of her. He was not empathic or sympathetic to her plight; he was simply tired of dealing with her situation. He finally granted the widow her request, so that he would no longer have to deal with her. Do you think it mattered to the Widow why the Judge granted her decision?

Luke 18: 1-8 (NKJV) states, ***"Then He spoke a parable to them, that men always ought to pray and not lose heart, saying: 'There was in a certain city a judge who did not fear God nor regard man. Now there was a widow in that city; and she came to him, saying, Get justice for me from my adversary.' And he would not for a while; but afterward he said within himself, 'Though I do not fear God nor regard man, yet because this widow troubles me I will avenge her, lest by her continual coming she weary me. Then the Lord said, 'Hear what the unjust judge said. And shall God not avenge His own elect who cry out day and night to Him, though He bears long with them? I tell you that He will avenge***

them speedily. Nevertheless, when the Son of Man comes, will He really find faith on the earth?"

This Parable also argues the benefit of prayer while being persistent by taking steps or action to further your desired outcome. Many of the commentaries discussed the meaning of the Parable of the Unjust Judge. Most of them say that this Parable demonstrates the benefits of continual prayer. That God will listen to you. But perhaps not only is it to encourage you to pray continually, but that actions based on your goals should follow prayer. Your actions should reflect your prayers.

Jesus Christ told his Disciples to "keep asking, seeking, and knocking." The word "keep," is often overlooked. Yet, it is significant. To keep means to do it continuously. Certainly, more than once or twice. Not that God is not listening the first time you ask, but by talking to God, you build your relationship with him. He will guide you and make known his direction or purpose for you through the ongoing relationship with him. We are not to be defeated with God as our guide. In Matthew 7:7-12 (NKJV), Jesus said to his Disciples, ***"Ask, and it will be given to you; seek, and you will find; knock, and it will be opened to you. For everyone who asks receives, and he who seeks finds, and to him who knocks it will be opened. Or what man is there among you who, if his son asks for bread, will give him a stone? Or if he asks for a fish, will he give him a serpent? If you then, being evil, know how to give good gifts to your children, how much more will your Father who is in heaven give good things to those who ask Him! Therefore, whatever you want men to do to you, do also to them, for this is the Law and the Prophets."***

Did you know that Apostle Peter considered "persistence," a virtue leading to Christian character or godliness? The Apostle Peter became an outstanding teacher, and he sermonized the word of God. He said that patience, endurance with godliness leads to brotherly affection, and brotherly affection leads to love for everyone. He argued that those who are shortsighted, or blind forgot they are cleansed from their sins. In 2 Peter 1:5-9 (NLT), the Apostle Paul spoke on persistence by stating, ***"In view of all this, make every effort to respond to God's promises. Supplement your faith with a generous provision of moral excellence, and moral excellence with knowledge, and knowledge with self-control, and self-control with patient endurance, and patient endurance with godliness, and godliness with brotherly affection, and brotherly affection with love for everyone. The more you grow like this, the more productive and useful you will be in your knowledge of our Lord Jesus Christ. But those who fail to develop in this way are shortsighted or blind, forgetting that they have been cleansed from their old sins."***

The Bible says so much about the benefits of perseverance, making it difficult to select those verses that are particularly special. There is one that should not only encourage you, but it should serve as a reminder as to who has created you. Isaiah 40:29-31 (ESV) says, ***"He gives strength to the weary and increases the power of the weak. Even youths grow tired and weary, and young men stumble and fall; but those who hope in the Lord will renew their strength. They will soar on wings like eagles; they will run and not grow weary, they will walk and not be faint."***

In conclusion, do not be discouraged when faced with starting over. Be persistent! Be reminded by Lamentations 3:22-24 (ESV), which says, ***"The steadfast love of the LORD never ceases; his mercies never come to an end; they are new every morning; great is your faithfulness. 'The LORD is my portion,' says my soul, 'therefore I will hope in him."***

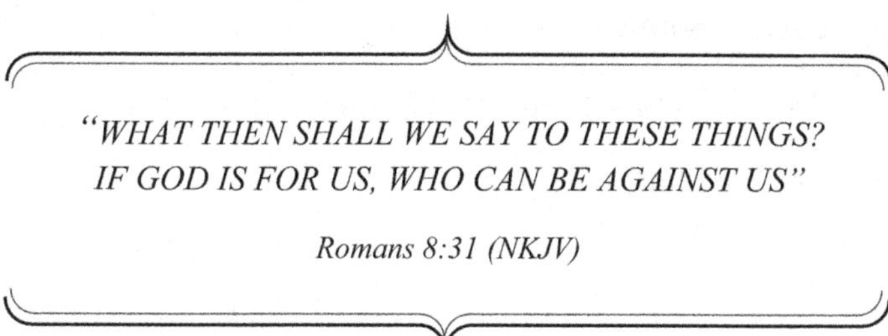

"WHAT THEN SHALL WE SAY TO THESE THINGS? IF GOD IS FOR US, WHO CAN BE AGAINST US"

Romans 8:31 (NKJV)

MY TESTIMONY

I was sitting in my bedroom reflecting on the past year. How was I able to start over? My father, who was both wise and witty, had died. My spouse had a stroke and two amputations. My mother fell, breaking her shoulder bone and injuring her hip. I believed I was denied justice and equity, while forced to watch my properties taken and my personal character undermined. To say that these past few months were rough does not adequately reflect my anguish, pain, and heartache. This is my testimony. I may have been bent, but I was not broken. Thank you, God!

MY FATHER'S DEATH

Shortly thereafter, on February 17, 2020, my father died of a stroke and pneumonia. The circumstances of my father's death were extremely unusual because prior to his death, both my father and my spouse were in the same hospital at the same time. They were on the same floor, doors apart. When family and friends would visit, they would take turns going from room-to-room.

I watched my father die. The hospice's doctor told me point blank that my father's condition would not improve. In fact, they turned off his monitors that reflected his oxygen levels. She told me they were going to change his room. There was an area in the hospital that allowed them to give a particular medicine to assist with his comfort level. I agreed, and she left the room. When transport came to move him, I was not ready. I thought the doctor meant sometime down the road, not right then. The doctor came back into my father's room and said a room was ready. I was not ready! I panicked. I needed time to reassess my decision. I knew what my father told me. He was ready to go. But I was not ready. My Aunt, my friend, sat with me in my dad's hospital room. It was as if he knew my panic and fear. The guilt associated with allowing my dad to die was heartbreaking. As I agonized over the decision. Sitting and watching him. He took one long breath, followed by a second, smaller breath. He died. He died before my eyes. It was not as I expected. He was at peace. I continued to watch him. A nurse walked in to check his blood pressure. She was confused when she couldn't get it. I told her he had died. She checked and called the doctor.

MY SPOUSE, MY COMPANION, FOR TWENTY YEARS

My spouse had been down the hall from my father. He had been suffering with sepsis and other types of infections from his foot ulcer. The doctors had amputated two of the toes. Then they amputated half of his foot. My father died on Monday. While I was planning for my father's funeral. I received word from my spouse that he would undergo a below the knee amputation on Wednesday, February 19, 2020. I remember leaving the funeral home where I was planning my father's funeral and driving to the hospital to kiss my spouse and give him some last words of encouragement. I could see fear on his face, but there was nothing I could do for him. He had been in the hospital from October 1, 2019, through April 12, 2020. When I say hospital, I really mean to say in the hospital, released to rehabilitation facility; back to hospital and released to rehabilitation hospital; back to hospital and released to rehabilitation; and back to hospital and released to rehabilitation, then home. If you were trying to count each cycle, let me just tell you. There were four cycles of Hospital to Rehabilitation Center from October 2019 through April 2020. He suffered with sepsis, gastroparesis, seizures, various infections, kidney issues, blood flow issues, etc.

COVID-19

By the end of February 2020, Covid-19 made its way to the United States and to the east coast. The news media described this disease as a killer. It killed the elderly and those individuals that are immunocompromised. It was in the air and on surfaces, but you could not see it. You, your family or friends could be carriers, but not know it. I was in a state of panic. I believed I was already suffering from depression, but this did not help.

There came a time that I was not allowed in the hospital to see my spouse, and when he was sent to the rehabilitation center in the middle of March 2020, I could not visit him. I would drive to the rehabilitation center, park near the side dumpsters and walk around to his room and poke my head in the screen at the window with our ten-pound dog, Pup Pup. I could hear and see him. He was always happy that we came to visit. I would bring him food or clothes from home.

One day, while visiting my mother, a gentleman was outside of her building and told me his wife was in the same facility as my spouse. In fact, their rooms were on the same wing of the facility. He told me that the Anne Arundel County Health Department was at the facility the day before and that they were experiencing a Covid-19 outbreak. I had just listened to the local news about another facility, Pleasant View Nursing Home in Mount Airy, Maryland, who had a substantial outbreak of Covid-19 and several of their patients had died, and a lot of the patients were suffering with Covid-19. I called the Anne Arundel County Health Department and spoke to an individual that provided the same information that I could see on the Health Department's website, but nothing more.

MY FRIEND AND ASSISTANT

An attorney who I sold my client list contacted me to inquire as to my assistant. She had become ill while working in his office. He wanted to know if she contacted me. I reached out to her, and she complained she had been to the doctors who thought she had bronchitis. She had a temperature, and her cough would not stop. She was miserable. I was concerned, however; I knew that over the years; she had suffered from various types of sinus infections and allergies, but this was different. She explained she was up in New York for a celebration about two weeks prior to getting sick. She said that she did not know anyone who had gotten sick, but every day, we were hearing reports about the Covid-19 outbreak in New York. I told her she should go to the hospital. She said she would.

In fact, later that evening, her new husband dropped her off at the hospital. No one was allowed in the hospital with her due to the new protocols in place to prevent the spread of Covid-19. Her daughter called me to say she had Covid-19. I could hear the panic in her voice. I called her husband to offer encouragement; however, I was not very encouraged. They moved her from the local hospital down to John Hopkins. Time moved slowly. There came a time when I spoke with her. She told me about her ordeal and how frightened she was at that time. She said that they were talking about incubating her, but she refused because she did not know anyone who survived on a breathing tube. She also said that as soon as it looked necessary, she took a turn for the better. She prayed.

I just face-timed her recently. She showed me her weight loss, which was significant. She teased me, stating that she had been working out regularly because Covid-19 likes fat, and she did not want to be attractive to it. I was proud of her weight loss!

MY SPOUSE

Finally, my spouse was released from the rehabilitation center on April 12, 2020. Because we lived in a 55 and over condo community, he had to self-quarantine at a nearby hotel for fourteen days before returning home as a precaution. It is my belief that the time at the hotel allowed my spouse to come to terms with his new reality and mourn without my interruptions. During that time, Maryland's Governor, Larry Hogan, had all the nursing homes and rehabilitation centers list information concerning Covid-19. It turned out that by the end of April 2020, the rehabilitation center where my spouse had been had approximately 95 people infected with Covid-19 and 13 had died.

When my spouse arrived home, he had various appointments with occupational therapist, physical therapist, foot doctor, vascular doctor, dialysis, etc. The good news was that after the amputation of his right leg, he learned how to use his prosthesis quickly and could walk and drive.

MY MOTHER'S FALL

On the Fourth of July 2020, I met with a friend that morning. I called my mother, but she had not answered. In the afternoon, I came home to pick up my spouse and drove him to his favorite Ethiopian grocery store. He picked up supplies to make his favorite Ethiopian dish. We also stopped to pick up the vegetarian portion of his meal at a nearby restaurant. The drive is about forty-five minutes from home, so I called my mother again. I knew I was going to stop at a seafood restaurant, and I wanted her to think about what she would want so I could order it for her. She did not answer the telephone. By this time, I was getting concerned. Sometimes, she did not answer her telephone, but usually she would call back.

On the way back from the Ethiopian store and restaurant, we stopped at one of my favorite seafood and soul food restaurants for carryout. I called my mother again, but she did not answer. I was with her the day before and knew she was doing well. I also understood my thirty-year-old was with her after I left. Usually, I call her several times a day. She is my mother; I do not need a specific reason to call her. Sometimes, we talk about what happened during that day, a television program, bible study, a friend or family member, etc. Sometimes, we fuss and talk later, only to fuss again. I love her even though we fuss all the time. Since she did not answer the telephone, I chose a fried catfish dinner for her. (Yes, I know it was the Fourth of July, however, I knew she would like catfish!)

As we were leaving the restaurant; I made plans to see my youngest niece; she had just adopted a Yorkie. Just by chance, I told my spouse that we should drop off my mother's food while it was still hot. When I arrived at my mother's apartment, everything looked normal. When I opened the door, I heard her call out my name. She sounded happy. However, when I walked into her bedroom, she was on the floor, trapped between her bed and the dresser. She had been there for over sixteen hours. She told me she had fallen. She said her shoulder and hips hurt terribly.

I immediately called the ambulance. When they arrived, they could not move her because of the injuries and the narrow space. They called for a second ambulance that had the necessary boards to help her move. I was scared! But she was alert, talkative and trying to crack a joke. Not only did I feel scared, but guilty, too. Should I have checked when she did not answer the telephone sooner?

My mother spent a couple of days in the hospital. The Nurse called me from the hospital to say that they would release my mother in a few hours. While on the way to pick up my mother, the Nurse called me back to say that she should be released to a rehabilitation center because she was having difficulty using her legs and that the left shoulder was broken. (I know what you are thinking. They should have known this prior to releasing her.) But because of Covid-19, I was afraid to have my mother in a Rehabilitation Center, so I told the nurse that I had her clothes and that I left them at the receptionist's desk. I told the Nurse to please get her clothes and put them on her. Afterwards, please bring her to the patient drop-off and pick-up; I was waiting for her to take her home.

I did not know what I was doing, but I was terrified of putting her in a rehabilitation center. First, due to Covid-19 restrictions, I could not see my mother. Second, due to my experiences with the last location my spouse was in before coming home, I did not want to expose my mother to Covid-19 by putting her in a Rehabilitation Center. For better or worse, I became her nurse.

I did not know I could not move her until we arrived home from the hospital. The young man who works in maintenance helped my mother from the car to the wheelchair. It looked easy. When I got her to her apartment, we were both relieved. When I tried to transfer my mother from the wheelchair to the bed, both my mother and I were stuck on the bed for a second or two. I did not have the strength that I thought I had at the time. I called my thirty-year-old, who came quickly and lifted her into the bed. For the first week, he stayed with my mother. He helped move her. While I tended to her needs. I would give her the medicines, clean her up, get her dressed, etc.

The second week, my thirty-seven-year-old and his father came. His father's wife had suffered a massive stroke, which left her wheelchair bound. Therefore, he knew what to do for my mother. He knew how to lift her and move her. Caring for my mother was much smoother by the second week. However, there came a time when they had to go. I said my goodbyes, looked away, and cried. I did not know how I was going to get through the third week.

When I arrived back at my mother's home on Monday morning, I had a surprise. My thirty-seven-year-old drove from Annapolis, Maryland to Cleveland, Ohio to drop off his father on Sunday. During the night, he had driven back from Cleveland, Ohio to Annapolis, Maryland and was resting in her living room when I walked through the door. I was so happy. He stayed for an extra week, but that week was significant. My mother and I figured out how to maneuver out of bed. After the third week, my twenty-seven-year-old and thirty-year-old would each come over at night to help get my mother in bed.

My mother was using her legs again. She could stand, though not for long, but she could stand. She could not use her left arm. And her pain levels had decreased. The fall had terrorized her. Lying on the floor for sixteen hours created a fear and uncertainty that would take time to heal and question her independence.

AGAIN, MY SPOUSE AND COMPANION

While I was tending to my mother, I received a call from my spouse. He had rushed himself to the hospital. His foot was bleeding profusely. (Remember, he only has one foot since the below-the-knee amputation in February)

It started all over again! The vascular surgeon explained legs are like twins. He said that what happens to one will probably happen to the other. I had hoped my spouse would have at least a year before he would have to deal with any major health problems. Hopes dashed! They took his big toe from his left foot. They took all of his toes from his left foot. They took his left leg below the knee. Have you wondered what it must feel like for a six-foot-eight man to lose both legs? How do you go on when your identity is tied to your height? When that which makes you, you no longer exist? I was afraid for him! This occurred right after John Hopkins called to say that they were removing him from the transplant list because of his coronary artery disease and the peripheral artery disease. When hopes are dashed, can you form new hopes? When all looks lost, is there still purpose?

The answer. He must start over! I must start over! We must start over!

BANKRUPTCY FILING

Has anyone ever tried to crush you? Was that person someone whom you expected to give you a helping hand? Were you denied fair access to the laws of the land? That happened to me. It has taken me six years to speak my truth. I was depressed and had anxiety for the longest time. I almost had a nervous breakdown. I even considered suicide. Questioning my life. Questioning my purpose. But my testimony only comes from the testing of my faith and my belief that there is a bigger plan for my life. A plan that I am not controlling. It is my belief that the best way that I can be an intercessor for someone else is to stand for truth and justice. To prevent what occurred to me from happening to someone else.

The Black Lives Matter movement and other groups that are tackling the inequity crisis in the United States seem to be concentrated on the criminal justice system. Those issues affect life and death of minority and poor people. The most pervasive issue is the ones involving wrongful deaths by police officers. Those that are called to serve but injure and kill instead. The other issue is the fact that the courts give minority and poor defendants harsher sentences than their white counterparts. The laws that are written to protect continues to fail under the biases of the courts. My case does not center on the criminal justice system. My story reflects the discrimination and partiality that I suffered in the civil courts with money as the motivating force.

There were only two questions that were at issue in my bankruptcy to me. By raising these questions, they attempted to crush me. Five white men against the lone black women. I was the rape victim who was made to feel guilty for wearing the skirt that so tempted and invited the rapist. This is the problem. The rapist is responsible for the rape, no matter what his lurid thoughts might have been. Only the rapist can control his actions. The skirt isn't an invitation, nor in my case, to seek help is not a time to be crushed. The following contains the background, the two questions and the punishment. Justice is not always Just.

BACKGROUND

After I graduated from law school in 1993, I worked for two mortgage companies in the early nineties. By 1995, I started my mortgage company. I obtained a warehouse line which allowed me to finance my own loans. I sold those loans on the secondary mortgage market. By the early 2000s, I invested in commercial properties that I converted into mixed-use units and a historical multi-unit dwelling.

Do you remember when the housing market collapsed in 2008? George W. Bush was the president. Senator Barack Obama and Senator John McCain stop campaigning and came to the white house to discuss our countries' financial future. One of the largest banks and financial institutions, Lehman Brothers, went out of business. The availability of capital came to a halt. People were laid-off. Real property depreciated across the country. This was the great recession of 2008/2009.

I was caught in the middle of the mess. I owned a mortgage company. Yet I could not provide a mortgage to my clients. I owned multi-use real estate. The properties were not breaking even. Unfortunately, I used all the cash I had to renovate the historic multi-unit property. I was behind on everything. I owned a total of four properties. My home, the historic mansion that contained twelve units and two four units in Laurel. I had no other income other than the rentals. Several of my tenants were hit hard by the economic collapse. Many were not able to pay their rent. My cash flow was dismal.

In 2009, I filed a Chapter 11 Bankruptcy in the U. S. Bankruptcy Court for Maryland in Baltimore. I hired an attorney. It is my belief that his total cost was approximately forty-five thousand dollars. He prepared all of the documents and pleadings. He attended motion and confirmation hearings. For those of you who do not know, a Chapter 11 allows you keep your property by working out an agreement with your creditors to pay them over a specific period. Sometimes, if the creditor disagrees with the proposed plan or settlement, the court can decide.

It is important to note that for bankruptcies, schedules are required. These are documents that contains your identification, property exemptions, assets, liabilities, income and family budget. The person who is filing the bankruptcy can complete these documents. In fact, in each federal courthouse, there are individuals who volunteer to help people filing bankruptcy. They cannot give legal advice, but they can provide the know-how as to a successfully filing.

My bankruptcy case was approved, better yet confirmed. It was approved despite the fact that I did not have sufficient income. I was able to modify (change) the terms of the financing on the properties in Laurel. The term was for four years, with one additional year. It was intended to run for the same period as the bankruptcy.

CALLS AND CONTRADICTIONS

After my bankruptcy confirmation in 2011, I received telephone calls from various people. The first call was from a man who stated that he bought my mortgage note from the liquidation sale of assets held by Greenpoint Mortgage Company, a division of Lehman Brothers Assets. Several other callers inquired as to my intention with the historic mansion. I contacted my attorney due to the unusual nature of the calls. He agreed the calls were highly unusual since the asset, the mortgage note on the historic mansion, should no longer be a part of Greenpoint. After all, Capital One Bank appeared in my court proceeding and held out the fact that they had the legal rights to make any and all decisions as to this debt.

My telephone calls turned into emails from men representing two different companies. They each made various claims about the ownership of the debt. Because of the confusion and a short payoff, I sought to refinance the debt on the historic mansion. Due to the bankruptcy, I could not find financing for the property. I moved to dismiss the bankruptcy case. The attorney for the mortgage company opposed the moved. The case was heard. The Judge stated I had done a good job. He granted my request.

The day after the court granted my motion for dismissal, the purported mortgage lender on the historic mansion send letters to all the tenants of the building demanding that they pay the lender directly, which eventually prevented any possible refinance of the property. This set up a legal battle. It also forced me back into bankruptcy.

I completed my bankruptcy schedules and first day pleadings for a second Chapter 11 bankruptcy. I later hired an attorney who I had known in the industry. In fact, he even wrote a book about Chapter 11 bankruptcies. He amended my schedules and attended one meeting; he came to the Meeting of the Creditors and the meeting with the U. S. Trustee that occurred on the same day, in the same room, one after the other. Shortly thereafter, I received one email. He did not return my telephone calls, nor did he respond to pleadings filed by my creditors. I spoke to the attorney who helped me initially, and he said to protect yourself, so I filed responses to the creditors. There came a point in time in which my attorney asked to withdraw from my case because I answered the pleadings. There is one lesson I know, do not allow someone who does not want to represent you, to represent you. Even if it is the night before a hearing on a motion to convert a case, which it was.

FIRST QUESTION

The first question is whether the mortgage company on the Laurel properties agreed to modify the properties for five years; four plus one which was concurrent with the term of the confirmed bankruptcy plan versus three plus one, a total of four years?

A. Email dated Thursday, September 23, 2010 from my attorney to me. He states, "*Attorney for Creditor* just called me to tell me that he has not had a chance yet to read my letter . . . He wanted to let me know that he is not ignoring us. . . I gave him the "thumbnail" sketch of our proposal. . . (Because you will probably remain in a Chapter 11 for 5 years and we would need time after your discharge to refinance even though we will continue to do that . . ."

B. Email dated Tuesday, November 2, 2010 from my attorney to me. The subject line states, "*Lender* agrees to 4 + 1." It continues by stating "*Attorney for Lender* will be sending an email to confirm this..

C. Email dated November 2, 2010, my attorney states, "I will have to prepare an Amended Plan containing all of the agreed terms with Lender. This may take an hour or so..

D. Email dated December 2, 2010, from Lender's attorney to my attorney stating, "Hope all is well. According to my diary, a Third Amended Disclosure Statement has to have been forward yesterday."

E. Email dated Wednesday, February 2, 2015, my attorney wrote to me, "We have received 2 Ballots from Patapsco Bank - both accepting as impaired classes..

F. Email dated March 6, 2011, Lender for Creditor gave my attorney permission to speak on his behalf at the confirmation hearing, which suggests that not only was there an agreement, but Lender's attorney trusted my attorney to convey the meaning of the agreement.

G. Attorney for Lender sent the modification documents to my attorney on June 30, 2011, and stated that the enclosed documents are for the modification, which contains the terms that were previously agreed to and included in the confirmed Disclosure Statement.

The Lender at issue had their own problems. They had to sign a written agreement with the Federal Reserve Bank of Richmond and the Maryland Commissioner of Financial Regulations because of their financial dealings. They made this agreement after a Task Force Report listed various discrepancies, complaints and other issues by this lender. The Board of Governors of the Federal Reserve System, Federal Deposit Insurance Corporation, National Credit Union Administration, and the Office of the Comptroller of the Currency issued interagency supervisory guidance addressing issues related to Troubled Debt Restructurings ("TDRS") This Lender was to be sold!

SECOND QUESTION

The second question is whether the evidence submitted against creditor on historic mansion was significant to prove they did not have standing or if it was merely hypothetical. Evidence is a sign which shows that something exists or is true. Also, evidence can be presented to the court to help find the truth about something. And standing is whether the party before the court has the right to be there. In my case, are they the note holder and if so, why not prove it with the document?

In today's world, entities hide behind other entities. Companies own companies. Therefore, the courts have held that documents filed with the agency responsible for the administration and enforcement of the federal securities laws, the United States Securities and Exchange Commission, (SEC) can be valid evidence.

U. S. Bank, as National Association as Indenture Trustee for Waterfall Victoria Mortgage Trust 2011 SBC3, appeared in my bankruptcy case. Can you tell what entity is hiding behind the other entity just be looking at its title?

What is a "Trust"? Wikipedia states that a trust is a legal relationship in which the owner of property gives it to another person or entity who must keep and use it solely for a third party's benefit. Let's look at the word "Indenture." It is a contract between parties. For example, an agreement to management the property for a fee. One party pays for the services of another. A Trustee is a person or entity that is placed in position to manage the property for the best interest of those they represent. In my case, U. S. Bank, is managing the mortgage note. For example, they are collecting payments or hiring attorneys. They are working for a company that is in the form of a trust called "Waterfall Victoria Mortgage Trust 2011 SBC3."

Who is "Waterfall Victoria Mortgage Trust 2011 SBC3"?

In some cases, trusts are so small that they are not recorded with the United States Securities and Exchange Commission. In fact, you may be required to become a financial detective in order to identify the actual owners, parties, members, etc., of a trust. In my case, on January 6, 2015, a company called, Sutherland Asset Management filed what is called a S-11/A document with the SEC.

I know you are wondering who or what is this entity? It turns out Sutherland Asset Management company was changing their business structure. They had their assets audited and sworn to by various owners of their company, legal department, and accounting. It turns out that they are the owners of Waterfall Victoria Mortgage Trust 2011 SBC3. The entity behind several entities. This is important because it goes to whether they have standing to be in the U. S. Bankruptcy Court in my case. It turns out that the audited and sworn statements says "no." They did not have standing to be there.

a. SEC FILING - The S-11/A filed by Sutherland Asset Management contained a list of all of their subsidiaries and Waterfall Victoria Mortgage Trust 2011 SBC3 is included in that list.

b. NO VALUE/NO ASSETS/NO LOAN - Page 317 of 419 in the S-11/A filing by Sutherland Asset Management states, "Waterfall Victoria Mortgage Trust 2011 – SBC3 as of September 30, 2014, that the Current Principal Value was "$ 0.00" and the Weighted Average Interest Rate was "0%."

c. TRUST COMPLETED BEFORE PURCHASE OF LOAN - Page 386 of 419 in the S-11/A filing by Sutherland Asset Management states, "Waterfall Victoria Mortgage Trust 2011 - SBC3 ("WVMT 2011-SBC3") is a grantor trust securitization completed by the Company in 2011.

d. TRUST NEVER INVESTED IN MARYLAND PROPERTIES - Page 386 of 416 in the S-11/A filing by Sutherland Asset Management reflects a table under Note 8 that shows real estate acquired in settlement of loans by state for the Waterfall Victoria Mortgage Trust 2011-SBC3. As of December 31, 2013, there were no mortgage loans acquired in the state of Maryland.

One of the follow-up questions before the court was simple. If Waterfall Victoria Mortgage Trust 2011-SBC3 was a grantor trust closed in 2011, it had no value, never acquired property or other assets in the state of Maryland, how are they before the court in Maryland in my case stating they are the holders of my mortgage debt? Especially when the legal instruments are backdated. I recognized the fact that backdating contracts are not necessarily illegal, but legal instruments. I argued the documents were fraudulent when it misleads a third party or gives a false impression about when an action was taken and the intentions of the parties are also important:

e. Assignment of Deed of Trust and Security Agreement from Waterfall Victoria Master Fund, Ltd to Waterfall Victoria Mortgage Trust 2011 SBC3 was "BACKDATED" for over two years. They signed it December 11, 2013 and Effective, October 19, 2011

f. Assignment of Endorsement of Deed of Trust Note from Waterfall Victoria Master Fund, Ltd to Waterfall Victoria Mortgage Trust 2011 SBC3 was "BACKDATED" for over two years. They signed it December 11, 2013 and Effective, October 19, 2011.

g. Assignment of Leases and Rents from Waterfall Victoria Master Fund, Ltd to Waterfall Victoria Mortgage Trust 2011 SBC3 was "BACKDATED" for over two years. They signed it December 11, 2013 and Effective, October 19, 2011.

Based on the above evidence, why wouldn't a reasonable adjudicator investigate the truth of the matter asserted when the above is sworn to after an audit and when the following are missing?

h. The governance for the Waterfall Victoria Mortgage Trust – 2011 SBC3 was missing.

i. The referenced "Loan Sale Agreement" was missing in the Assignment of Deed of Trust from Green point Mortgage Funding, Inc. to Waterfall Victoria Master Fund, LTD which is dated June 23, 2011.

j. The Loan Sale Agreement is missing from the sale by Capital One Bank as successors by mergers to any entity that received the note.

k. Missing authority that GreenPoint Mortgage Funding, Inc. had ability to transfer a debt that they did not own, even if it is now a division of Capital One Bank, it must reference its authority, which it does not.

l. The Proof of Claim, document to prove indebtedness in the bankruptcy court, which was filed by U. S. Bank, NA did not have any endorsements, assignments or allonges from Capital One Bank or Lehman Brothers.

m. There was a high profile lawsuit between U. S. Bank, NA suit and GreenPoint Mortgage Funding, Inc. alleging fraud. It stated that the business of GreenPoint Mortgage Funding, Inc. was to structure, originate and sell but not to service the debt. This was significant to my case because Lehman Brother was the owner my debt and not Greenpoint Mortgage Funding.

n. I received a letter of transfer of the debt as well as 1098 Mortgage Interest Statement and Escrow

> Statement from Lehman Brothers. As alleged by U. S. Bank NA lawsuit, my debt was only originated by Greenpoint Mortgage Funding but transferred to Lehman Brothers shortly after origination.

I realize that for someone who does not finance real estate transactions. This may be hard to understand. But think of it this way. You took out a loan on your house. In exchange, you gave your home as collateral. The note represents the debt, the amount of the loan. The deed of trust represents the collateral, the house. The note and the deed of trust becomes legal documents, legal assets that can be transferred and sold for money. More often than not, the transfers or sales are generally to business entities, including trusts. When a sale takes place, there is a paper trail that follows. In order to sale your note and deed of trust, the party that is making the sale must own the debt and have proof of ownership. Sometimes, there is no proof of ownership, therefore, they may not have the right, or standing, to sell the debt. Or the party they purchased the debt from them did not have the right to sell it. Why is the issue of standing important? It goes to the heart of collection. Who has the right to collect your mortgage payments? Legally, is it the one that shows up in this transaction or is it the one that has the legal documents allowing them to collect. My argument was simple, who has the legal documents to collect? In my case, the response is that I was looking for a free house. Similarly, it can be said that the entity that is hiding behind other entities is looking for a free income stream or assets to sale?

MY PUNISHMENT

Understanding the two questions that were at issue is to understand the argument that I raised repeatedly in my bankruptcy case. But they castigated me for raising these issues. It was almost as if I was the rape victim, whose character was destroyed because she wore a skirt. And the defense argued the skirt tempted and invited the rapist.

Discovery is a method that can be used to seek information from the opposing party, entities, or persons of interest that may provide additional information and evidence. In my case, several entities hid behind restraining orders granted by the court and others failed to provide all the information requested. The creditors did not respond to my objections to their "Proof of Claims," which are documents filed by creditors stating how much they are owed and what is the basis for the debt.

Intimidation is a technique that can crush an ideal or claim. In my case, the Trustee and the Creditor accused me of a felony for using my own funds of approximately three hundred and fifty dollars, $350.00, while in Arizona. They called it a "shopping spree." When I filed my plan and disclosure statement, I used as a draft the plan and disclosure from my first case that the court approved. There was language that stated we reached an agreement. I made an error by rushing to file a plan and disclosure statement since my attorney was not responding to pleadings. I was told that the error was meant to deceive the court. These accusations had a cooling-off affect which was meant to intimidate.

I like to use the term "coloring the books" when the creditor, trustee or attorney paint a picture that is not true. A pleading called a "Motion to Lift Stay" allows the creditor to be move jurisdiction out of the federal bankruptcy court. There are several reasons lender may prefer another jurisdiction. In Maryland, only state courts can foreclose. In my case, the Lender on the Laurel properties filed a motion to lift stay on the properties stating that I was in default while returning my regular monthly mortgage payments back to me. This happened for three months. During this time, the lender's service department sent me a check stating I paid an overage into the escrow and they were refunding me the money.

Several months later, the Lender withdrew that motion and filed a Motion to Lift Stay seeking foreclosure arguing that the loan had ballooned. They argued that since the loan had ballooned, there was no avenues for the court but to grant their request. I continued to argue that I had not received the applicable time as stated in the modification documents, but to no avail. After my case, I represented a lady whose husband had died. He had a reverse mortgage on their home. Time had run out, and she had not provided the required documents to the lender as the spouse. They sought foreclosure against her, making the argument the mortgage had ballooned. I used an exception and prepared a plan to allow her to stay in the home. It was approved.

When testimony, witnesses and other evidence is not allowed, a record of the case can not be build for purposes of an appeal. In my case, I attempted to appeal but soon learned that if the issue was not heard in the lower court, there is nothing to appeal in the higher court. Only the judiciary allows what evidence or who brings it in!

Apparent ex parte communication between the Trustee, Creditor and the Judge. At one of my hearings, the Judge came out of his chambers and as we sat down, he belittled me by saying, “Ms. Smith-Scott, you would not let them into your unit?” I had to ask him what he was talking about. But it was clear, the U. S. Trustee, the attorney for the Chapter 7 Trustee and the Judge looked at one another after I responded to him. There had been no testimony that I was a part of concerning entrance into my business.

When the Trustee, Attorney for Chapter 7 Trustee and Judge refused to allow me to buy out my estate, which is a bankruptcy term, allowing for payments to creditors versus the sale of property. This allows the person in bankruptcy to keep their assets, but to pay its value to the trustee. At one point, the Judge stated he would not want the creditors to be burdened with me because of my attitude.

They denied me the right to put forth my opposition to the sale of my real property. My expert that I paid to fly from Florida to Maryland was not allowed to speak or testify. She could not offer her findings even though she was a fixture in the bankruptcy courts.

The attorney for the Chapter 7 Trustee argued I did not have an interest in the sale because there would be no proceeds or monies that would be of benefit to me. The attorney for the chapter 7 trustee failed to disclose my financial responsibility as to the agreements that he reached with the creditors. He failed to say that I would have a tax liability on more than a half a million dollars. Years later, I was notified by the Internal Revenue Service that I had gains on the historic mansion in the amount of approximately three hundred and eighty thousand dollars, $380,000.00. And on the Laurel properties I had gains in the amount of $180,000.00. I was not provided a copy by the creditors or the chapter 7 trustee of the forms filed with the IRS.

The Attorney for the Chapter 7 Trustee came after my business, which was not party to the bankruptcy. My business had a separate tax payor identification number and was independent of me. First, they garnished my bank accounts without my knowledge and without court authority. Second, although my business had a lease agreement, they sought the eviction from the business from the premises. This building had two residential tenants and two business tenants, yet they came after my business and its tenancy.

In violations of the laws of Maryland, the creditors, with the assistance from the Attorney for the Chapter 7 Trustee, had property managers to collect and move the tenants from the residential units. In fact, there came a time in which they turned off the water on the premises to force tenants out.

The attorney for the Chapter 7 trustee went before the court to say that I was intimidating and harassing my tenants after the property managers had taken over for months. This statement was believed and accepted by the court even though I was the legal representative for several of my tenants.

During the proceedings, I received three orders stating that I was in contempt. They all centered on the Laurel properties and the fact that my business, a separate entity, would not move from the location.

In front of the Trustee and the attorney for the chapter 7 trustee, my case was ruled non-dischargeable. There was no true hearing with live testimony. There was simply an accusation and the ruling. This meant that they sold all of my properties, took my monies and that I would still be responsible for all the debt that remained.

I sued the Chapter 7 Trustee and his attorneys. I stated that they intentionally breached their fiduciary duties while representing the estate; were negligent while representing the estate; and how their actions amounted to gross negligence, which caused financial and emotion injuries to the Plaintiff. Shortly after this filing, the Attorney Grievance Commission received an anonymous complaint against me, which eventually led to my disbarment. The only witness that the Attorney Grievance Commission brought against me was the attorney for the chapter 7 trustee that I sued.

It turns out that the Attorney Grievance Commission can use what happened as the basis for disbarment, but any actual facts in opposition to the complaint are considered "re-litigation." My attorney told me to apologize and to move forward. I threw myself under the bus trying to save my bar license. It is inherently unfair to raise issues but not to address the issues that are before you.

I was disbarred in the state of Maryland. I was licensed in the Federal courts as well. You must have a state license in order to practice federally. However, the federal courts allow time to show cause why you cannot continue, and their process is not immediate. However, on the day of my disbarment from the state of Maryland, in all of my federal cases, my hundred plus bankruptcy cases, received a docket entry followed by a notice that I was suspended or disbarred. I could not turn over my cases in a manner that was best for my clients. I did not have any time to speak to them. It created a dark cloud. I had not been reprimanded in federal court. My federal court license had been recently renewed with no problems at all. Yet, the office of the U. S. Trustee made this decision going against the rule of law.

Not only had the office of the U. S. Trustee made this decision to enter this statement, but they also stopped payments on all of those clients whose cases they confirmed already or during that month. This meant I had already done the work. I was waiting for payment from the bankruptcy trustees. This equated to about twenty-five thousand dollars, $25,000.00.

And if this was not bad enough, the case was written about publicly with the emphasis of an attorney who represented herself that made misrepresentations to get her disbarred.

STEPS TAKEN SEEKING RELIEF FROM INEQUITY

Several appeals were filed. The first appeal was on the order granting the motion to convert from a chapter 11 bankruptcy to a chapter 7 bankruptcy which was filed by the lender on the Laurel properties. It contained evidence that was not discussed in the lower court. The ruling was not overturned. I started over by trying to get evidence on the record, but was unsuccessful.

A motion to remove the Chapter 7 Trustee for Cause pursuant to Title 11 of the United States Code, Section 324 in accordance with Federal Rule of Bankruptcy Procedure 7052, made applicable under Federal Rule of Bankruptcy Procedure 9014. It was denied.

A motion for recusal of the bankruptcy judge pursuant to Title 28 of the U.S.C. § 455, Title 28 of the U.S.C. § 2106 and the Federal Rule of Bankruptcy Procedure, Rule 5004. It was denied.

A motion to move the entire bankruptcy case pursuant to 28 U.S.C. § 157(d), District Court Local Rule, Rule 402 and Federal Rules of Bankruptcy Procedure, Bankruptcy Rule 5011. It was denied after more than a year.

Prior to the bankruptcy filing, a twelve-count complaint was filed against the alleged lender on the historic mansion. This case was dismissed after the Chapter 7 Trustee filed a motion stating that they were the only one entitled to move forward with the case. They reached an agreement with the Lender where the Chapter 7 Trustee would receive a portion of the proceeds of sale.

Almost a year after the bankruptcy filing and months after the conversion from a Chapter 11 to a Chapter 7 Bankruptcy, a complaint was filed against the lender on the Laurel Properties. It alleged fifteen (15) counts. The case was dismissed, too, after the Chapter 7 Trustee filed a motion stating that they were the only one entitled to move forward with the case. They reached an agreement with the Lender where the Chapter 7 Trustee would receive a portion of the proceeds of sale.

Last, I showed up. It was discouraging. Humiliating. But I showed up. In fact, shortly after my hearing on the issue of non-dischargeability, the Judge, his friend, the U. Trustee, and the Chapter 7 Trustee retired.

PROFITABILITY OF THE CHAPTER 7 TRUSTEE

When many people think of bankruptcy, they think of poverty-stricken individuals. It is hard to understand how much money is really at play. Donald Trump filed bankruptcy several times. The benefits to him were much greater than the judgment of anyone else. There is real money at play. The chapter 7 trustee is to represent the creditors and their income is derived from several sources. First, they receive a percentage of what is collected. The greater the income, the greater the money that they receive. Second, the chapter 7 trustee hires an attorney, usually someone who is in their firm. How many hours at what hourly rate? It is exorbitant. Third, they hire real estate agents who are generally related to their firm. And fourth, they may hire their firm to act as an expert in a matter. In other words, they receive commissions, attorney fees, agency fees, etc. In my case, they received almost two hundred thousand dollars. But that does not include attorney fees or real estate related fees. Being a chapter 7 trustee can be a profitable business.

COST OF SEEKING HELP

Yes, I was found in contempt. Injustice breeds contempt. I never thought that in seeking help to reorganize that I would be denied the access and use of the laws that I used to help others. These things happened because I was attempting to fight it alone, not seeing the pattern of abuse or the monies necessary to fund an opposition. Especially after hiring an attorney who disappeared when the fight started. He returned a small sum.

I got physically sick fighting this case. I could not sleep. And, I had severe anxiety. It has taken some time for me to heal from the trauma of this experience.

Bent, but not broken!

HOLY CITY AND BIBLE STUDY

Let me tell you a story. My maternal grandparents attended a church in Ebenezer, Mississippi called "Holy City." It is a small church. It is a real small church compared to the mega churches of today. In fact, prior to Covid-19, this church only opened for one Sunday each month. I believe the local Pastor rotated between several small churches each month. Since Covid-19, Holy City Church has not opened for that one Sunday each month, instead, they have bible study and church service through a free conference call provider. Monday through Saturday, the Bible Study is by 11:00 AM and on Wednesdays and Sundays, the program is by 6:55 PM.

My mother loves Bible Study. My aunt (I have been told my whole life that I act like her, look like her, and sound like her and whom I love dearly) loves Bible Study. The gentleman who began this outreach is a charismatic and knowledgeable family friend who has known my mother and aunt since childhood. He recruited my mother, my aunt, my first cousin/sister and a host of people he knows to participate in these bible studies and church programs because he loves bible study. In fact, he has a very unusual story. When he was a baby, he was left at the front door of a lady who lived closed to my grandparents. She loved him and raised him as her own. (He has since discovered his real parents.)

My mother, being a busy body and not believing that I have the ability to read the bible, requested that I take over from her as a facilitator for Bible Study. Her argument was that each person should be given a chance to facilitate and since I was not working right now, it would be an opportunity for me to learn the bible and have something that we could share. Well, I really was not interested in participating in Bible Study and I believed I have shared my whole life with my mother and there was no need to have another "common interest" with her. After all, we shared my father, her husband; her sister, my aunt; numerous grandchildren; adopted grandchildren and church members; etc. We lived next to each other for years and we took vacations together. How much more sharing of "common interest" could she want from me?

Reluctantly, I decided to facilitate one Thursday, replacing my mother. I studied, investigated, read articles online, listened to various YouTube programs on the subject matter, prepared notes, long notes. I was ready to facilitate. Did you know the bible is a lot like reading a textbook? The Bible requires actions. It tells you stories, but you must be able to apply those stories to your life.

Problem: I pondered on the many questions I have for God! I am mad, disappointed, overwhelmed, scared, etc. You know, God has a lot to answer for.

Solution: I will ask those hard questions of the various participants, maybe someone will have the answers. They should be smarter than me. In my quest for understanding the Bible and its principles, I noticed that I have changed.

Bible Study changed me! I think it can change you too.

"ASK, AND IT WILL BE GIVEN TO YOU; SEEK, AND YOU WILL FIND; KNOCK, AND IT WILL BE OPENED TO YOU"

Matthew 7:7 (NKJV)

CONCLUSION

There is so much to say about "Starting Over." It is my hope that the sixteen steps will help encourage and inspire you to start over. It is difficult, but you can do it. I have discovered that the steps can help you arrive at your goals. They have helped me.

The first step, "Acknowledge the times and Do Not Let Frustration Set-In," asks you to consider whether this may be the time to rest, reflect, and restart your life. You have an opportunity to live an adventure, to do something totally different. Incorporate a plan of action. But first, you must recognize and accept where you are in life so that you can concentrate on your next steps. Frustration will only hinder you.

Step two states, "Do Not Let Your Past Destroy Your Future." Was the past really that great, or is it we now know the outcome, which reduces our anxiety? When faced with something new, it forces us to risk our time, talents and maybe, money too. Not knowing the consequences brings uncertainty about the future. But we can't allow the past to stand in our way. Time is continuing to move forward, whether we like it. We need to be thankful for our past and look forward to our future.

The third step, "Love Yourself, Openly, Freely, and Joyfully" for you are "fearfully and wonderfully made." Your characteristics, your strengths and weaknesses set you apart; it is what makes you unique. Loving oneself begins with accepting oneself. It means that you recognize and approve of that which makes you, you. The power of love is said to be one of the most significant forces in the universe. Use that force for the good within you!

Step four states, "Forgive Yourself, Live a Guilt Free Life." Forgiveness is the act of pardoning an offender, and that includes pardoning yourself. This allows you to let go of guilt and blame. It is easy to become frustrated and disappointed when you believe you have done your best, only to fail. But remember, Jesus Christ has died for your sins, which nullifies your guilt and blame. He has forgiven you. Therefore, let go and forgive yourself.

The fifth step, "Step Out in Faith," relies on one of the most repeated bible verses, which is Hebrews 11:1. It says, ***"faith is the substance of things hoped for, the evidence of things not seen."*** Faith must be tested. For it is the test, the suffering, that refines who we are and examines our belief and strength. We are shielded through faith given by the power of God which protects us. Remember, it takes faith, as little as a mustard seed, to move mountains.

Step six says, "Pray for Wisdom and Seek Guidance," for God is your personal compass. Prayer is an intimate communication with God.

Keep in mind, there are many benefits to a powerful prayer life. God's word is a shield. God's word will bring peace. God's promise is fulfilling and satisfying. God's word allows for personal growth. Rejoicing in God brings you Glory. God's word changes you. Do not forget to ask the Lord for direction before taking any action.

The seventh step, "Listen and Wait on God," requires that you be attentive and focus on God. Distractions can stand in the way of our ability to hear and understand the word of God. From the time man was created, God has been trying to get our attention. He has used various methods to speak to us. There are consequences when we do not listen.

Step eight says, "Set Up a Joy Plan." This is a plan of action that purposely seeks to bring joy to your life by taking actions that will uplift you, change your attitude, and help you grow as a person. Have you changed and not realized it? When was the last time you had a "hearty" laugh, not a giggle, but laughed until you cried? A joy plan does not have to cost you money, but it requires that you consider your needs and dedicate some time for you.

The ninth step, "Expect a Blessing," states that you should believe that you will receive God's protection and favor. A blessing comes in many forms, including psychological, physical and spiritual. Physical blessings are those that include food, drink, and shelter, so that we can maintain a safe and secured life. While spiritual blessings are those things God gives us for our spiritual being. It is a term meant to express the fullness of God's gift of eternal life in Jesus Christ. For Christians, expectation is the belief that they will be blessed.

Tenth step says, "What is Your Value?" We are seeking to place a dollar tag on our value, but when something is priceless, how can it be valued by man? Our value is not on how we compare to someone else, but on how we compare to ourselves. Each of us has our own identity, history, and experiences. It is my belief that to value yourself based on your title, income, or position is a fool's folly that leaves us unsatisfied, unfulfilled, and useless. Our value comes from God. He thought we were so valuable that he sent his only begotten son to live among men, die for our sins, and was resurrected. Sending the Comforter and giving salvation. We must be valuable to God for such a sacrifice.

The eleventh step, "Blessings from God," defines a "blessing" as the act or words of a person who blesses, who conveys a special favor, mercy, or benefit. We are blessed in ways that are impossible to consider, because our blessings are both known and unknown. Jesus Christ shows true blessings are not related to the accumulation of things or powerful people, but of the characteristics that make a difference in someone else's life. Our greatest spiritual blessing is the gift of salvation, everlasting life.

Twelfth step says, "Be Grateful, Gratitude." Our chances for success increase when our outlook changes for the better and we show gratitude. We should be grateful, thankful, and appreciative of what we are given. Gratitude comes with many benefits. It is a partner to both Faith and Hope. It acknowledges that God is present in our lives. It expands our spiritual blessings. It reflects our appreciation to not only God, but to others. It encourages other people to want to reach out to us. It can extend your longevity. It can increase your joy of living. The list is too numerous to include, but gratitude justifies blessings.

The thirteenth step, "Intercession, Helping Others," which is the act of intervening on behalf of another. It follows the mission of Jesus Christ, who said that the greatest commandment is to love the Lord with all your heart, soul, and mind and love your neighbor as yourself. It has been documented that volunteering helps to change the body's physical response to stress through lowering blood pressure and reducing inflammation.

Fourteenth step says, "Not Really a Step, Remember to Write it Down." There are many benefits of writing things down, things like your goals, dreams, and aspirations. It's an excellent way to express yourself, to state your fears or desires in a private setting. It allows you to get things off your chest, protecting you from unnecessary or unwanted confrontations. It helps you make affirmations for yourself. It helps you remember tasks and chores. It assists you with strategizing and planning. It's a good way to memorialize events and/or activities. It serves to verify or confirm actions taken in the past. It's a great way to communicate; express your feelings or thoughts toward someone else. Helps you accomplish your goals. Take the time to write it down.

The fifteenth step, "Stay Encouraged, It Can Be Hard." We all need encouragement, someone in our corner. It offers hope, provides much needed reassurance, and changes an attitude or outlook. It allows an individual to confront an issue that may appear to be overwhelming. Encouragement can be the nemesis to fear. Hope, Faith, and Peace can be the benefactors of encouragement while inspiration is the product of encouragement.

Sixteenth step says, "Be Persistent," which is the ability to keep on getting up. The benefits include a greater chance of reaching your goals. It allows you to think outside of the box. And it tests your endurance and strength. Persistence is a virtue leading to Christian character or godliness. Remember, Jesus Christ told his Disciples to "keep asking, seeking, and knocking."

I am giving you a challenge, hoping it will help you take your first step if you have not done so. My challenge is that you write your testimony. This is your chance to look at your yesterday, to look at the past, and to reflect. While you are working on your testimony, it is my hope that you will begin the step of starting over while relying upon the Lord for your direction.

I Pray that You and Yours will have Mercy and Peace! Live your Adventure.

THE END

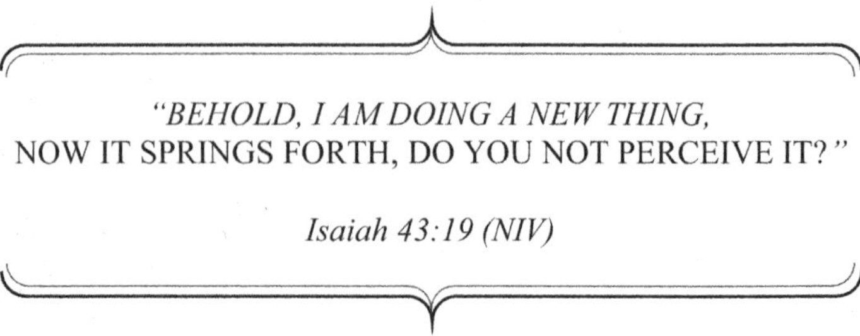

"BEHOLD, I AM DOING A NEW THING,
NOW IT SPRINGS FORTH, DO YOU NOT PERCEIVE IT?"

Isaiah 43:19 (NIV)

GOD IS DOING A NEW THING

One day, I began to write. Before I knew it, I wrote this book. I seemed to be inspired. It was not until the editorial process did I think I made a mistake. I wanted to share the various bible verses and stories that I liked the most, but I had not considered how many of them I included in the book. I guess I got carried away. The process became time-consuming. Also, I realized I made many errors. Almost every other hour, I would hear myself say, "What was I thinking?" Nonetheless, I persisted.

After I completed my first draft, I sat down and began to write again. This time, a fictional story. The story is called, "Finding Peace." The story began with the main character seeking drugs from a doctor. The character's life is similar to my own, but not the same. She, too, was anxious and depressed. While she waited for the doctor, she felt a presence in the exam room. First, she thought it was her imagination, but then she realized that something or someone was there with her. She tried to run from it, only to get home and find him waiting for her. He took her to Heaven. It turned out that she was an invited guest to witness the judgment of man. Along the way, she met people who would become her friends and their lives would change forever. But had the tribulation begun? Is the book of Revelations unfolding before her eyes? What role would she play, if any?

I have included an excerpt for your review because God is doing a new thing in me!

EXCERPT FROM

"FINDING PEACE"

I

The Search for "Drugs"

How do I ask this doctor for "drugs" without telling her the whole story? I should have rehearsed my lines. Now, I am sitting in the doctor's office. Placed in an exam room with the door closed. I heard the bump when the nurse placed my chart on the outside of the door. There's muted talking. I hear someone on the telephone. I can't make out the conversation. I glance around the green room. It is a dreary green but there is a small window bringing natural light into the room. There are posters on the wall. One poster features a medicine for Type-2 Diabetes. The couple that is on the poster appears to be happy, per the poster. The couple have their diabetes under control with the medicine that is advertised. The other poster has a diagram of the neurological system of the human body. I am wondering, is that what I look like without skin? The weird things that come to my mind these days. I continue to look around the room. There is a small desk, one chair and a stool, an exam table and cabinets with an antiseptic wash, glass container with cotton balls, another glass container with Q-Tips and a third glass container with the small packages of the sterile wipes. There is an old fashion blood pressure monitor and other equipment attached to the wall. I stand up and look out the small window.

This is a new doctor for me. I want her to prescribe "Xanax" for anxiety, however, it actually helps me to sleep, too. My previous doctor prescribed both "Xanax" for anti-anxiety medicine plus an anti-depressant, but it was only for a short period. He explained he was prescribing .25mg of Xanax for two weeks because it took about two weeks for the anti-depressant to work. He said that "Xanax" was addictive, so a small amount for a short time was all that he will prescribe. Once I took the "Xanax," I found myself less anxious. My mind was calm. I thought, why bother taking the anti-depressant when the "Xanax" worked so well.

Sitting. Waiting. Looking at my phone. This room must have been cleaned before they placed me in it, because it still smelled like bleach. Should I open the door? . . . Checking my emails instead. My mind is racing. My thoughts are all over the place. I have not slept for more than a few hours a night. Either I am running to the bathroom, or I am replaying the past. I cannot sleep.

When had the tide turned? When I was young, I was invincible. Especially when I was on my roller skates! Thursdays were adult nights at the local skating rink. You had to be twenty-one years old and older. Tuesdays were for teenagers and Sundays were family night. I thought I was the world's greatest roller-skater. My skates stayed packed, and I was ready to roll. You could not tell me anything. Confident. I was self-assured and confident.

When I moved to Washington, DC, from Cleveland, Ohio, I was also self-assured and confident. I remember telling my parents that I was moving. It came as a surprise to them, so they said, but that could not be true. My mother tells the story of when the two of us went with our church, St. Peter's Church, to Washington, DC on a bus trip. I was a child. I do not remember how old I was at the time. She said that every time we were let off the bus to see a landmark, a monument, a museum, etc., I was always late coming back to the bus because I was exploring, trying to see everything. She said that I had no fear and knew my way with no problems. What she left off is the fact that I fell in love with Washington, DC.

A few years after that trip with the church, I took a train from Philadelphia, where I was visiting my aunt, to Washington, DC, to meet my two half-brothers, William and Thomas. There was never talk about my two half-brothers. In fact, I did not know that they existed until I was fourteen. However, in our family's old photo album, there was a picture of a couple cutting their wedding cake. The groom looked like a younger version of my dad, however; the bride was not my mother. It turns out that the groom was my oldest half-brother, William. I got his number from my father. I called William and said, "I am your sister and I want to meet you!" Both William, Thomas and Reynold, an adopted half-brother, met me at Union Station. They drove me around Washington, DC, and to Georgetown. They were loving and considerate towards me. It never occurred to me that our meeting would not go well. I never had a doubt. I never second guessed the call. I was confident.

When I announced, I was moving to Washington, my parents panicked. I was the youngest of their three children, and I was eighteen years old. They had invested their hopes and money in me. But I refused to go to college after attending Symphony School for Girls. It was a college preparatory high school, yet I wanted to do something other than "School." At the time of my announcement, I had recently finished basic training and AIT, Advanced Individual Training, in Fort McClellan, Alabama. I was a 95 Bravo, military police in the Army National Guard.

When I made the announcement, my father made a deal with me. He said I could move to Washington, if by the end of the week, I would have a job. Specifically, he said that he would drive with me to Washington, DC. While there, he would visit with his Mother, his cousin and his three sons. He would visit for one week. When he was ready to leave, if I did not have a job, I would have to come back home with him. After one week, I had three job offers. I accepted the position as a stockbroker in Georgetown. The only problem with that job was that you had to be twenty-one years of age or older, and I was not. It was not until my orientation, after my father went home, did I discover the age requirement. The company really liked me. They hired me to be a secretary. It took them a day to realize I really could not type. My manager took me to lunch at a swanky restaurant nearby and fired me. I got another job and stayed in Washington. I was confident.

I was out on a date with a neighbor, a man, from my apartment building, when I met the man who would become my husband. I loved to dance. In fact, I thought I was the world's greatest dancer. However, my neighbor enjoyed drinking and watching other people dance. He would not dance with me. I told him I was going to ask someone else to dance. I noticed my husband (not my husband at the time) watching a table where five women were sitting. As he made his move towards the table, I intercepted him and asked if he would dance with me. We danced the night away. When I was ready to leave, I realized my neighbor had gone. I am not sure when he left because I was having so much fun dancing. He was the driver, and he left me stranded. My Husband took me home. We sat outside my apartment talking for hours.

I do not think my husband actually proposed to me. It is my recollection that I said that if we were still together a year from then, we should buy a house together. Once he agreed, I suggested we get married. He agreed. I made my plans. Confident.

I stood up and looked out the window. I am growing impatient. Where is the doctor? I hear laughter in the hallway. There must be something funny, however, I am not in on the joke. No, I am sitting in the exam room waiting for the doctor to come. Patience was never one of my virtues. I am still trying to figure out how to get the doctor to prescribe Xanax without asking too many questions. Really, I need to sleep the entire night. Really, I need some peace. I need to let go of the past.

II
PEACE OR A PIECE?

Peace. My mother is always hollering she needs peace. When I was young, way before my sister died and when my brother was still living at home, we were arguing and fighting amongst ourselves. We were loud and disruptive. I do not remember what the fight was about now, but my mother ran around the house with Crisco oil, not the liquid oil that you see today, but the old can of Crisco oil, the shortening. My mother was praying to the Lord for "peace," while throwing bits and pieces of Crisco oil around the house. In her words, she was rebuking the devil. The three of us; my sister, brother and myself, slowly stopped arguing and watched our mother. She was loud. And she was funny. We eventually went outside. I wonder if that was the "peace" that she was seeking?

I am seeking peace, too. But what is "peace"? I guess that is why I am sitting in this doctor's office. I hope she can prescribe "peace." I worry about everything. Literally. Will I get Covid-19? Will my friends or family members get Covid-19? Are my kids safe? Will they be treated fairly on their jobs? Will there be enough money to get through this crisis? What will life hold tomorrow? Should I sue? Am I prepared to facilitate bible study? Does my mother have enough to eat? Drink? Did I get all of her supplies? Did I pick up her medicine?

I don't remember when this unrest began for me. Was it when the housing bubble burst, causing my business to close? Was it when those that I expected to be fair, turned out to be condescending and unfair? Was it the fact that my beloved father died? Or the origination of the invisible disease that can steal and kill without prejudice? I have been estranged from "Peace." Or should I say, I lost my "Peace of Mind."

I wonder will "peace" stop me from thinking about everything? Does peace lead to substance abuse? Recently, my niece made rice crispy treats with marijuana. She said, "Auntie, just break off a little before you go to bed. It will not get you high, but it is going to make you feel relax." I had it in my purse for the longest time. Sometimes at night, I will pull it out and look at it real hard. Frequently, I would open the plastic bag and smell it. One night, I even broke off a piece, but it is still in the bag.

My nephew said that I should try some CBD oil. In fact, he had a little container with a small brown cigarette, not your typical cigarette, but one that is rolled. He said, "Auntie, this is CBD oil. I want you to try it." He pulled out his lighter to show me how to light it. I promised him I would try it. It is still sitting in my kitchen, waiting for me. Why do I think a prescribed drug would be so much better for me than the kid's suggestions? You would believe that a professionally trained individual would be more apt to know what they are doing when it comes to prescribing medicines. Right? I had to think about that proposition.

I looked up from my telephone. I thought I saw something in the corner. I could not quite make it out. I thought I felt something. My imagination running away with me. I stand up, stretched, and opened the door. I glanced down the hallway. All the doors are closed to the exam rooms. Miscellaneous noise coming from behind the doors. I looked up the hall and I can see someone, a part of someone, back of their head, their left shoulder and back. She is sitting at the desk on the phone. The door to my right is the bathroom. I might as well use the bathroom before the doctor comes to my exam room.

Back in the exam room. I am wondering what time is it? I look down at my phone for the time. There it is. That feeling again. The feeling that someone is here with me. I wonder if the nurses or the doctor are spying on me. See, I really need some Xanax. My anxiety level is high. Even I realize it. There was a time that I was considered "calm," "reflective," "thoughtful," not now. Yes, I need the Xanax.

Didn't Whitney Houston die of a Xanax or a combination of alcohol and Xanax? Let me look that up quickly on google. Yes, on February 13, 2012, NBC News did a report that Xanax and alcohol may have killed her. There is a report from TMZ the day before that said Whitney Houston took Xanax before her big shows. ABC News broke her coroner report down on April 5, 2012, they reported, "A "plethora of prescription medication bottles" were found in the room, according to the final report. The final report lists 12 different medications, including anti-anxiety medication Xanax, and muscle relaxer Flexeril, prescribed from five different doctors." Wasn't I prescribed "Flexeril" when my back was hurt?

"Why are you here? Your help does not come from man or things made by man!" I looked up. I glanced around the room, past the window, the posters, the exam table, the counter, and by the door. I looked for an intercom and the telephone line. I got up. I opened the door. I turned to my right, down the hall. I turned to my left; the person is still on the telephone. I listened for noises, only voices coming out of the other exam rooms. I checked my cellphone. It did not appear as if I had not butt dialed anyone, either. Did I actually hear someone speaking to me? What did he say, "***Why are you here? Your help does not come from man or things made by man!"*** I am really hearing things. Am I going crazy?

I walked to the end of the hallway, where the nurse was sitting on the telephone. She looked up at me and covered the phone. ***"Can I help you?"*** She appears to be in her early forties. She is the color of caramel, and her hair is in a bun. She is polite, but she is firm. I asked her if she knows how much longer it will take for the Doctor to come to my exam room. She says that the doctor had an emergency that has caused her to be delayed. She is not sure how long it is going to be before I am seen by the doctor. She said that I was the third person or the third in line, waiting to be seen. The person on the other end of the telephone is saying something to her. She glances down at the desk and speaks into the telephone. The Nurse tells the person that the doctor had been waiting for confirmation of the test results for the last half hour and that she needed the information urgently. I walked back to the exam room. I leave the door open.

III
PEACE, NOT SUICIDE

I paced for a moment. I am torn. On one hand, I think I should just reschedule and come back at a later time. While, on the other, I really need the rest and I need something to calm me down a bit. Being new to me, the doctor may prescribe Xanax as I requested, so I am reluctant to leave. Looking around the room again, I sit down on the stool. I used my cellphone again. There is an article that states that people use Xanax and alcohol, or other combination of drugs to commit suicide. The World Health Organization states that approximately 800,000 people die because of suicide every year, which is one person every 40 seconds, and that it is a global phenomenon. The National Institute of Mental Health states that suicide is among the leading causes of death in the United States. In 2018, the Centers for Disease Control and Prevention issued a report which included three findings. First, the report says that suicide was the tenth leading cause of death overall in the United States, claiming the lives of over 48,000 people. Second, the report says suicide was the second leading cause of death among individuals between the ages of 10 and 34, and the fourth leading cause of death among individuals between the ages of 35 and 54. And, third, the report says that there were over two-and-a-half times as many suicides (48,344) in the United States as there were homicides. So, for 48,000 suicides, there were 18,830 homicides.

There are other articles that say more people than ever are suffering from fear, depression, anxiety, loneliness, substance abuse, alcoholism, and other forms of mental health issues. In fact, suicides are on the rise and the coronavirus just makes it worse. After reviewing those articles, I feel depressed.

As I sit there, I remembered how I felt "that" day. I woke up saying to myself that this will be the day. I laid in bed. I held on to Princess and cried. She was so warm and loving. I can't imagine something so little could bring so much joy. Still, she was not enough. I knew she would be loved. When I finally got out of bed, I looked out the window. It was a dreary day. It looked as if it rained during the night. I could not tell what the temperature was outside, but it did not matter.

Should I take a shower or brush my teeth? It, too, did not matter. I put on some clean underwear but wore the same jeans and shirt from the day before. I walked Princess one last time. I fed her and hugged her. She gave me a funny look before I closed the door. She seemed to sense what I was going to do. I walked down the hall, rode down the elevator, and walked around my neighbors who had gathered near the elevators. Several of them inquired about my spouse. I smiled and said he was "fine" as I hurried past them by and went out the side door.

Once in the car, the music from the radio blared, causing me to jump. I plugged in my telephone and went to YouTube. I searched for something to listen to while I drove, but could not make up my mind. I opted for the radio. As I turned out of the parking lot, I thought about what I was going to do. I was about ten miles from the Bay Bridge. It is a long bridge about two-and-a-half miles long. I thought the timing would be perfect. It was after rush hour, so traffic should be light. I listened to the music as I drove. I passed the signs for Route 2, Bay Dale Road, Sandy Point Beach, slowing down to go through the tollbooths. To my surprise, the tollbooths were no longer there.

I slowed down to merge onto the Bay Bridge, making sure I stayed in the right-hand lane. My heart beat hard and fast within me. I could feel it. I became fearful considering my next moves after all. This was the day. As I drove slowly going over the bridge, I looked for the jump-off point. I knew it was midway. I saw it the day that I took a dry run. I questioned myself, "Are you sure you want to do this? Really?" As I was pondering this question, I drove even slower. Tears rolled down my face. When I finally got to the jump-off point, I slowed all the way down, almost coming to a complete stop. I grabbed my purse, my keys, and my telephone.

That is when I noticed a red pickup truck behind me. It honked. I tried to ignore it. As I reached for the door, the driver put all of his weight on the horn. I did not know what to do; the noise was distracting. Then the driver, a middle-aged white man, drove his pickup truck around to my driver side door. He rolled down his window and hollered, "YOU ASSHOLE, GET A LIFE!" As he drove off, I sat there stunned until I saw a car in my rearview mirror driving up on me at a fast pace.

I drove off. Before I knew it, I was on the other side of the bridge. I stopped and ate at Cracker Barrel. As I waited for my French toast, I replayed in my mind what occurred. The Driver said, "Get a Life!" It was at that moment that I realized I would not commit suicide. I was not going out like that! I wondered, why did I grab my keys, phone and purse to jump off of a bridge? I laughed and cried while I ate my French toast. The server came to the table to make sure that I was okay. I told her I needed to get a life. She smiled, not sure what to make of me.

Isn't it funny, you never know what is in someone else's mind? Growing impatient, I continued to review the articles on mental illness, wondering if I was suffering from it, too. I always known mental illness was a problem, but to the extent that it exists, it is unbelievable. What is surprising is that money and wealth do not alter the statistics surrounding suicide, in fact, people with money will still commit suicide at the same rate, if not higher, than a person without it.

On June 5, 2018, well known fashion designer, Kate Spade, died of suicide. She had a net worth of approximately $200 million dollars. She was a former editor of a fashion magazine, Mademoiselle. She created a fashion sensation in the 1990s with her line of accessories, including handbags, shoes, and accessories. I am wearing her shoes that I purchased from Nordstrom Rack. They are really comfortable. I wonder what made her want to end her own life.

They found Anthony Bourdain dead in his hotel room in Kaysersberg, France, on June 8, 2018. He committed suicide. He was a celebrity chef, book author, journalist, and travel documentarian. In fact, his job allowed him to travel all over the world and sit down with famous people, including Barack Obama, and eat great food. He had a show on CNN called, "Parts Unknown." I watched it occasionally.

On January 6, 2009, Reuters reported that German billionaire Adolf Merckle committed suicide. He was the world's 94th richest person in 2008. He built a conglomerate with over 100,000 employees. His family issued a statement saying, "The desperate situation of his companies caused by the financial crisis, the uncertainties of the last few weeks and his powerlessness to act, have broken the passionate family entrepreneur and he took his own life." I knew nothing about him, but to have hired 100,000 people is significant.

I loved Robin Williams. I loved him in Mork and Mindy. I loved him in Mrs. Doubtfire and Good Morning, Vietnam. Yet, he died by suicide on August 11, 2014. He was incredibly talented. He won the 1997 Academy Award for Best Supporting Actor for "Good Will Hunting," as well as two Emmy Awards, six Golden Globe Awards, two Screen Actors Guild Awards, and five Grammy Awards. It is surmised that at the time of his death he had a net worth of approximately $50,000,000 to $100,000,000.

I guess you never truly know how another person sees their life and their value to others. As an outsider, looking in, you always image what it feels like to have that life. The life with all the trappings. It must feel great. You can eat whatever you want, whenever you want, and you never have to cook yourself. You can hire a personal chef. You have the type of money that allows you to be free of the worries about the necessities, such as the mortgage payment, car payment, the credit cards, taxes, etc. In fact, you can write a check to cover the total cost with a blink of an eye. You are valued and respected. When people see you coming, they say "yes sir" or "no ma'am." The banks are fighting over your deposits, paying the highest rates possible and offering concierge services for their financial instruments. Concierge services can provide tickets for the best seats in the house, at the concert of the year, at a moment's notice. What a life? Yet, people still leave that life by choice.

I was watching Netflix. Dave Chappelle's show, "Sticks and Stones." He made a joke about wealthy people committing suicide versus an acquittance of his who lost everything. He described the incident in which he states that his acquittance was happily wearing an umpire uniform at the Foot Locker. David Chappelle said that his friend did not consider suicide. But that is the problem. Dave Chappelle did not know what his friend may have considered. You really never know what is going on in someone else's head. And clearly, money is not as satisfying as one would think.

IV
THE PRESENCE IS IN THE ROOM

"Why do you speculate on such matters, when Wisdom and Knowledge require understanding of the word of God." I stopped in my tracks. I raised my head and glanced around. I heard that voice clear as day. The voice was not deep, but definitely a man's voice. I jumped out of my seat and ran into the hallway. I looked at my telephone to see if I accidentally called someone. I glanced back at the exam room. I reviewed the window, the posters, the exam table, the cabinet, the chair, and the stool. No one was there. I checked the telephone that was sitting at the desk. I was spooked. I know I talk to myself, but that was not my voice!

You know what? I do not need Xanax . . . today! I walked up the hallway where the nurse was previously sitting; she was no longer there. I followed the exit sign to the door. As I was about to leave, the receptionist stopped me. *"Ms. Evans, did the doctor give you any orders or prescriptions?" "Excuse me?"* I responded. Repeating herself, she said, *"Did the doctor give you any orders for blood work, prescriptions or a time frame in which she wants to see you back in the office?"*

I told her, *"No, I have not seen the doctor. I was told that she was running behind. I think I would just like to reschedule the appointment."* The receptionist says, *"She was behind. We really had a serious emergency here in the office. We are so sorry for the inconvenience. We would hate to see you leave when the worse is over and she is catching up, slowly but surely. Do you have something else that you have to do today, Ms. Evans?"*

I answered her. *"Yes, I have an appointment in a bit, and I am afraid I am going to be late. Can I just reschedule my appointment?"* She glances at her computer and says, *"Oh sure, let me see . . . okay, how about next Friday?" "I will take it."* I ran out of the office.

When I got outside, the heat from the sun hit me. I forgot it was a sunny day because the exam room felt so dark. I looked up to see the sky. From the corner of my eyes, I saw something or someone, but I am not sure what it was. I turn to look at it, but I see nothing. I realized that someone or something is with me. I feel a presence, a being, but it has not fully made itself known to me. Should I run to the police station? Where is the police station? My fat butt cannot run! I should have had the hip surgery like my aunt told me to do years ago. When I get to the police station, how will I explain that a presence is chasing me? Can you imagine what they will say to this old, fat lady who limped all the way to the police department only to say that a ghost is behind her? Would they believe me? I definitely think that I would get three days in the psychiatric ward.

Okay. Should I go to my car? It was right there in front of me. I walked towards my car. However, I am not alone. I mean, I can feel someone nearby, but I cannot see them. (Yes, my eyes are opened!) Quickly, I turned to go to the nearby Popeyes restaurant instead of the car. I moved fast and when I got to their door; I reached to open it. "Curbside Service or Uber Eats Only" Due to the Covid-19 pandemic, they are not letting anyone in the restaurant. I stood there, looking around, afraid to go back to my car. People drove past me to go to the drive-thru. I looked at them and they noticed me. I smiled, but they do not know I am smiling because I have my mask on. Now, my smile is really not a smile, it is a smirk. I am trying to figure out if I should holler "HELP." But what for?

I stood at the door to Popeye's restaurant for a while. I guess I looked suspicious because one employee came to the door and asked if I had placed an order or if I was with Uber Eats. I told her I thought I could come in and order, so I left my car at the doctor's office. I explained I would get my car and return going through drive-thru for my order. I walked to my car.

As I walked, I reasoned with myself. How ridiculous was I for thinking I heard a voice, not once, but twice? I was really silly thinking I saw something, better yet, felt something in that tiny exam room and then when I walked to my car. I laughed at myself for refusing to go to my car instead, running to Popeye's. At least, I could have bought a chicken sandwich. I felt better by the time that I opened my car door and sat down. I hoped the receptionist did not see me. Clearly, I was silly.

I hit the ignition button while I put my foot on the brakes to start the car. The radio came on. I sat there for a moment and relaxed. The telephone rang. It was my spouse. As I talked with him, I left the parking lot and made a right at the light. I got on the highway. I really missed being with him. He was in a Rehabilitation Center near our home. This past year has been really stressful for him. He was in the hospital from October 1, 2019, through April 12, 2020. He went back to the hospital in October

2020 and was transferred to the Rehabilitation Center. He is 6’8”. He has had both of his legs amputated. He suffers with diabetes. I think both of his parents died of diabetes or complications of diabetes. It is really a terrible disease. They say that it is a silent killer. What people do not realize is that it attacks the blood vessels, the kidneys, the heart and other organs of the body. Most people associate it with the lack of control of your blood sugar, not knowing the full extent of the damage it causes. He is on dialysis because his kidneys will not work. His blood flow is reduced to his extremities. His heart is weak. He has had a massive stroke. However, he is a fighter!

I did not realize how he would have to fight. In February 2016, I came home from work to find him in his bedroom face down on the floor. I hollered, “What are you doing on the floor?” I panicked, and that came out of my mouth. Our small dog, Princess, appeared to know that something was wrong with him. She kept on hitting him with her two front paws and jumping over his back and shoulders, trying to reach for his face. I thought he was dead. I was just about to call 911 when he moved. He got up on all fours for a minute, then he sat down, still on the floor, but on the side of the bed. He asked me “what was wrong?” I calmed down and let my nerves to settle. Again, I asked him why he was on the floor? I wanted to know if his back was hurting. As I was talking to him, I notice he would say, “What’s wrong,” “Are you okay” and “Uh, huh.” But not necessarily in a responsive manner.

He was still on the floor but leaning against the bed and sitting upright. I wanted him to get off the floor. I would ask him to get up. He would answer me by saying, “What’s wrong” “Are you okay” and “Uh, huh." I noticed his eyes were not all the way there, meaning he looked blank even though he was responding. I finally realized that he was not responding. He was saying the same thing over again. I told him if he did not move, I was going to call the ambulance. He continued to do and say the same thing. I called the ambulance.

When they arrived at the house, I let them in. The paramedics talked to him. His response did not change. They peered into his eyes and considered his face as they spoke to him. They took his vitals. His blood pressure was 200+ over some large number, -- too high! They got him on the cart and took him to the ambulance. I followed them to the hospital, parked my car, and ran to the waiting room in the emergency department. I told the intake nurse who I was and that my spouse was just brought there by ambulance. I had to wait for a few minutes while they were placing him in the exam room. The nurse took me to his room.

There were many people running around him. Vitals were checked and doubled checked. Hospital staff checked his eyes, his mouth, any movement of his body and searched for any obvious injury. They hooked up IVs so they could put medicine to reduce his blood pressure. Tests were ordered. Questions were asked and responses noted on the computer. They asked me what happened? As I explained, my quiet giant got restless and agitated. He pulled off his clothes. This, from a man who would not go to a nudie bar with me when we were in Miami Beach, Florida. This, from a man who did not want me to come into the bathroom if he was using it, after being together on and off for twenty years. He was no longer speaking. He pulled out his IV. The doctor said that he was in an altered state. That although his eyes were open, he was not seeing what was before him. Because of his sheer size, the nurses could not put the IVs back in him without restraining him. Nor could they get an MRI of his brain because it required that he not move, but he was moving whether it was voluntary or involuntary.

The nurses called in the security guards to help restrain him. During this process, something really funny happened. The security guards and the nurses were trying to hold him still in order to restrain him. During this process, he stood straight up. All 6'8" and 255 pounds of him. He went to the sink that was in the room and vomited. Personally, that gave me hope. He had to be aware of his surroundings, his brain was functioning. If his brain were not functioning, how would he have known where the sink was in the exam room, a strange room, a room that he was not familiar with at the time? After he vomited in the sink, he sat on the bed and allowed the nurses to do what they were doing. He laid back and closed his eyes.

Over the next three hours, he went from saying, "What's wrong" "Are you okay" and "Uh huh" to being totally unresponsive. The doctor believed that he had a stroke due to a lower brain bleed, but they could not verify it until an MRI was done. A stroke was not reflected on the MRI when it was finally performed. Eventually, he was moved out of the emergency department and to the hospital. I do not remember for sure, but I think they placed him in the Intensive Care Unit. There were monitors on the wall outside of the unit near the nurse's station. That period was like a blur. I would come to his room. His eyes would be closed, and he would be non-responsive. I would sit with him, looking at my telephone and watching television. I would talk with the nurses and the doctors who came and went from his room.

One morning, I received a call from the doctor. She said that it appears as if he was doing a little better. In fact, she thinks he could hear her and that he was responsive. She told me that when I arrive, I will see for myself. That encouraged me. I got dressed and went to the hospital. My hopes were high. When I walked in his room, he was looking at me, hollering, ***"Why did you leave me in this place?" "Why am I naked?"*** And ***"Did you bring me some clothes?"*** I was happy and not happy to see him awoke and alert. I was happy because the doctor was wrong when she said that he had a stroke or lower brain bleed. He was alive and aware of his surroundings. I was not happy to see him awoke because of his emotional state. He was confused, angry, and betrayed.

When I think about those days, I am happy that he is still here with me, but the doctor may not have been totally wrong. He has a hard time remembering the past, people and directions. However, he still remembers how to cook. And, he has a wonderful attitude about life. Our dog, Princess, simply adores him. Speaking of Princess, I knew she was waiting anxiously for me to arrive back home. During the last few months, we have spent our days and nights together. We were inseparable.

V

WHERE IS YOUR FAITH?

I am home. I am going through the list in my mind of things that I must do, beginning with taking Princess out so she can use the bathroom. The elevator makes the binging sound when the door opens and announces the floor. I open the door and walk into the condo, expecting to see Princess at the door. She is not there. I called her name while I put my purse down. By now, she would ordinarily greet me. But she does not come to me. I notice she is sitting in one of the two recliners in the living room, the one closest to the sunroom. I wonder why she does not come to me. I walk over to her, and I can see she is looking right at me. She appears to be happy to see me, but she does not move. As I reach down for her, I hear, in the same man's voice that I heard in the doctor's office, ***"Why are you running from "peace", while saying, you are seeking it?"*** I let out a heart wrenching scream, I panicked. The voice is coming from the recliner, but no one is there. Princess jumps down from the recliner and barks. I look down. She is barking at me.

Princess is looking up at me. She can tell I am in a full-blown panic. Her whole body is moving along with her tail. She is still barking. I am looking back at her, but I cannot control myself. I am getting hot. The room is spinning. I feel as if I am going to get sick. It is as if time stood still. Princess, she has stopped barking. Yet I am disoriented, confused and afraid. I feel like I felt when I passed out at Kaiser several years ago. As if I was fading to black. I am falling, but I have not landed.

"Where is your faith?" The voice is clear as day. Again, it is a male's voice. I do not know this voice. I mean, I recognized it from the doctor's office, but I had not heard it before the visit. I was afraid to look up. I do not know why. Yet, I do not feel like I felt when I was running from the presence. I was calming down. Princess is looking at me as if I am "the ghost" and not the man. She looks like she is trying to say, ***"Snap out of it!"***

I was sitting down across from the "Man," the ghost, who had been speaking to me. I was sitting in the recliner, but I do not know how that is possible because the recliners were on the other side of the room. In fact, my spouse and his sister both joked, what a waste of money to purchase recliners when they will not fit the space. I placed both of them next to one another at an angle in the corner, so you can get past to go in the sunroom, see the television or watch Matt play the piano.

"Where is your faith?" He asks me again. I considered his question. "Where is my faith?" Is that an implication that I once had faith? . . . Who is this man sitting comfortably in the recliner across from me? Why is he here? Why is he making inquiries of me? I should be the one to make queries of him.

I answered his question with a question, ***"Why are you sitting in my living room asking me these things? Who are you? What is it you want from me?"***

"Remember, how he told you, that one day you will be called to advance his purpose?" He waits for an answer from me, but that does not sound like an answer to my question. I do not know who "he" is talking about.

"I am sorry, I do not know who or what you are referencing." I pause as I make this statement. ***"Again, you are in my home. Who are you and what do you want from me?"***

He answers me. ***"I am a ministering spirit sent out to serve those who seek salvation. I am here to guard his ways."*** But I do not understand his answer. I think of the movie, "Rush Hour" when Chris Tucker's character asks Jackie Chan's character, ***"Do you understand the words that are coming out of my mouth?"*** I heard what he said, but I do not understand what it means.

"Where is your faith, the faith that allowed you to feel confident?" He asked me again as he considered me intently. I studied him and pondered the question. I was trying to figure out what he meant and what he wanted. However, I realized the answer he gave me is the answer I am going to get. As I replay the question in my mind, "Where is your faith?" I think of the old James Cleveland song called, "Where is your faith?" I think the lyrics of that song are actually a conversation between two friends. One that is down on his luck and the other one, who is trying to encourage him, ask him where is his faith? The song goes like this:

Say you've been sick?
Tell me about it.
And you've think you can't get well
Where is your faith?

Where is your faith in-God?

Say you're in trouble?
Tell me about it.
And you're going to court next week . . . and so on . . .

As I sat in the recliner, I felt a warmth, a calmness come over me. Princess, who was at my feet, left my side. She walked over to the man. I think he picked her up. She was not barking. I raised my eyes to look up at him. I wanted to know who is holding my dog!

He sat in the recliner opposite me, watching me intently. He was patient. I observed him, trying to get a clear picture of him. There is a light that surrounds him, making it difficult for me to see him well. I think I need to get up and turn off the lamp. It may be too bright for him. No wait, he is in my house. I do not know this stranger, why should I try to make him comfortable in my house? But is that right . . . Is he a stranger?

He was dressed in bright white with matching pants and shirt. If you have ever seen a paint chart for white, it would be the brightest of them all. Besides the color, there is nothing out of the ordinary. He is not bejeweled. No large jewelry, watches, necklace, rings, etc. I cannot quite make out his race or nationality. He definitely is not white. He could be black if he were mixed with something else. He could be Middle Eastern, Egyptian, Ethiopian, Iranian or Turkish. Is he Arabian? Is he Asian? My father would be ashamed of me. He loved sociology and geography. If he were alive, he probably would know his nationality with one or two looks. He is mature but youthful. He appears to be slender and fit. One thing I know for sure is that he is a man with a mission. What that mission is I do not know? He seems to be single-minded. But I no longer have any fear of him.

"When you were a child, your faith was limitless. Not only did you believe in our Lord, but you knew he blessed you with a guardian angel? What happened to that child?" He is speaking to me as if he had known me my whole life. Did he say, ***"our Lord?"*** . . . Is he talking about God? . . . I believe he is talking about me when he asks, "***what happened to that child***." I am thinking to myself. I really do not know what happened to her, "that child." Does he know I am old? No longer a child.

"Okay, what happened to you, old lady? He smiles. I smiled at him, too. I relaxed a little more. However, he speaks to me as if he knows my thoughts. So why does he ask me questions when he knows my answers? I remember facilitating a Bible study when Luke 9:37 was discussed. It began by saying, ***"Jesus, knowing their thoughts . . . "*** I still had not answered his question, but he lets me go through this thought process without interruption. Does he really know my thoughts?

Finally, I say, ***"Life happened!"***

He responds by saying, "***Jesus said to them, "I am the bread of life; whoever comes to me shall not hunger, and whoever believes in me shall never thirst." Did you forget John 6:35?"***

I decided just to be honest with him. I get the sense that he knows me, whether I know him. ***"No, I did not forget."*** I took a pause and began again. "***I guess I have gotten further away from the word of God*** as ***each day goes by. I do not know why or when the shift occurred. As I faced***

life's dilemmas, I relied upon my own understanding. As I experienced successes and disappointments, I tried solving my own problems; planned my strategy hoping to reach my goal." I took a quick pause. "***Maybe it was the small everyday actions and decisions, those that are hardly noticeable, that caused a shift away from the word of God and Jesus Christ. Yet, I know I need them."***

"You must learn how not to lean on your own understanding, but on the word of God," he says, responding to my statements. You know what the scriptures say, ***"You should, "Delight yourself in the LORD, and he will give you the desires of your heart. Commit your way to the LORD; trust in him, and he will act. He will bring forth your righteousness as the light, and your justice as the noonday."*** After a quick pause, he asks me the following, ***"Do you understand you cannot find peace because you are paying the penalty for your failure to rely upon the Lord? You are in a self-imposed exile."***

As he pets Princess, he laughs a little and then he says, ***"I have been watching you for a long time. There is a contradiction in you. You pray to God for help after you find yourself in a full-blown crisis. You pray after you worry yourself sick. Then you do not take heed to the call of the Lord. You know, you make it harder than it has to be, right?"***

I was stuck. His statement was a simple one, yet to the point. He is right. I have worried myself sick and waited until the crisis has suffocated me, then I prayed to God. It never occurred to me I behave this way, not until he actually said it.

As if he could hear my thoughts, he says, **"Do not worry about your life, what you will eat or what you will drink; nor about your body, what you will put on. Is not life more than food and the body more than clothing? O you of little faith?"**

Clearly, he is calling me "you of little faith." Have I lost my faith or am I afraid to act upon my faith? Are those the same questions or are they different? I wonder if he knows the difficulties of living in this world.

VI
THE VISIT

We sat quietly, watching one another. We did not have a stalemate. I think he knew I was going to give him the surface answers to his questions. They would neither be lies nor truths. The answer will contain omissions hoping to stay away from any conflicts, disagreements or harm. I really did not know if there was any need to answer him. I think he knew the answers to his questions already. The question was definitely rhetorical. "Why do I worry?" I guess it is the uncertainty of each step in this life.

While preparing for bible study, I ran across a sermon by a well-known pastor on YouTube. He was teaching from the book of Acts. He made a statement that I thought about while this man was sitting in front of me. He said that there are two questions that we should ask God. The first question is "Who are you, Lord?" The second question is "What do you want me to do?" Certainly, this "Man" is here for a purpose, and he said he was "sent" to me.

"Yes, those are the right questions to ask? Most people assume they know the Lord. Yet, they fail to understand all that he is and all that he does. Not only is he the Alpha and the Omega, the first and the last, the beginning and the end; God is spirit, and those who worship him must worship in spirit and in truth. God is love, and whoever abides in love abides in God, and God abides in him. He is the Rock; his work is perfect, for all his ways are justice. A God of faithfulness and without iniquity, just and upright is he. It is written, "I AM WHO I AM." There is so much to say, yet, I have said enough."

He stopped for a moment. I could see that he was not finished with his statement. ***"The second question, "What do you want me to do, Lord?" I was asked to come to you. You have been struggling, which has caused you to become both deaf and blind. You have not answered the call and you don't have much more time?"*** What does "You don't have much more time" mean? Am I dying tomorrow? Should I be getting my affairs in order? Who shall I call to say "Goodbye?" How will I die? Will I die of a heart attack? Cancer? Automobile Accident? Covid-19? How about all of this stuff I accumulated in storage? Who wants this stuff? Did I make a difference in this life? Why did I even live? He was right, I have been struggling! I stopped for a moment. He said that I have not "answered the call." ***"What call,"*** I inquired?'

His reply: ***"For I know the plans I have for you, plans for welfare and not for evil, to give you a future and a hope."*** He stops and starts again. ***"Who has been calling you Andrea?" Whose voice has been echoing through the wilderness? Whose voice have you heard in your dreams as you sleep, as you eat, as you drive down the road? Whose voice has been calling you?"***

This man is no ordinary man. He is not only single-minded, but purposeful, I said to myself. He was speaking to me, to my heart. He was quoting Jeremiah 29:11, which is a popular verse. Does the book of Jeremiah have anything to do with me? I quickly tried to remember what I learned about Jeremiah. God called him to warn the Israelites. He spent years telling them to be obedient to the word of the Lord, that they would be judged and punished. Eventually, the Israelites were punished through oppression by the King of Babylon for seventy years. After their captivity, the Lord instructed Jeremiah to write a letter telling the Israelites that God will come to them. In the meantime, they were to build houses and live in them, plant gardens and eat their produce. They were to take wives and have sons and daughters; they were to multiply. They were to pray to God for the welfare of the city, for the welfare that they find within the city will be their welfare. Finally, the letter ends with a warning to them. Beware of false prophets, for they will deceive them. They will use the Lord's name; it will be a lie, for the Lord did not send them.

What is this man saying to me when he spoke of Jeremiah? Is this a warning to be obedient to the Lord? Is he telling me not to listen to false prophets? Maybe this statement was more personal. Is he saying that I should accept my circumstance and that it would not be permanent? Similar to the idea of making the most of a bad situation. Should I be praying for my town, my city, my state or my country? That my fate is tied to its fate. Is he saying that people are lying when they say they are doing something in the name of the Lord? Who is "they"? He raised all types of questions. What is he actually saying to me?

"All the above." He started laughing at me. Clearly, he knew my thoughts. That is going to be a problem. "***I have been sent so that you will get a better understanding of the forces that are at work. Forces that are bigger than you and I. But keep in mind, God's thoughts are not our thoughts, neither are our ways God's way."***

I repeated him. ***"You have been sent so I will get a better understanding of the forces that are at work. What exactly does that mean?"***

"You are alive. Yet you act as if you have died. You have played with the notion of death, in fact, you have even considered it as an option. Over what, exactly? Because you have been treated unfairly, they took your property from you. Yet, food is still plentiful. You have continued to eat well; you have shelter, and you are loved. You have forgotten your many blessings. Do you understand that there are many people worse off than you?"

I shook my head "yes" however I did not believe it.

"Do you realize how many times you are under attack, but God's mercy and grace has prevented you from being harmed?"

Again, I shook my head, but this time, the answer was "no." I did not know.

Then he said. ***"He would like you to witness something."***

"Who is "He"? I wondered. Certainly, he is not talking about God. Is he?"

"Who else would I be talking about?" I have been asked to bring you to Heaven. You are to witness the trial of man."

"I am sorry. I don't understand you. Can you say that again? Heaven." I was puzzled. He did not twitch his nose or blink his eyes. But we were no longer in my living room.

VII
ARRIVAL TO HEAVEN

We are flying, but I do not know how that is possible. I am still in the sitting position; however, my chair is not underneath me. I am having an out-of-body experience. I am no longer contained within my body. I feel light as air! I am free as the wind. The feeling of weightlessness is amazing. I am reminded of when I was young. I was an excellent roller-skater. There were moments when I was on my roller skates that caused me to feel like I was flying. I haven't been on skates in years, but that was the only experience that I have had that caused me to feel like I was actually flying. Wow, this is simply wonderful. My movements are like a ballerina who is in the midst of their highest or longest leap. They looked as if they were flying. Maybe I am feeling like an astronaut who is experiencing zero gravity. It is fantastic.

The "Man" is to my left. He is smiling at me. We are traveling above the earth. I reach my fingers out in front of me and it appears as if they had become a part of the universe, no longer my fingers. I did zoomies in the air. It makes me think of my boxer, Bapsey. When I first brought her home, she did zoomies in the yard. She was so excited. I feel the way she felt. I am experiencing an explosion of energy and excitement.

My vision is limitless. As we continue to move towards the moon, the stars, and the sun, I look back and see earth. I watch it carefully. It spins ever so slowly. I see the continents, the oceans, rivers, and seas. The mountains and volcanos. I see smoke coming from enormous areas of the earth. I see people dying in huge numbers. I see the sick and the hopeless. I see how the animals on the earth are suffering. I see the rich living behind gated walls, while the poor struggles for a morsel to feed their children. As we move past earth, my energy and excitement levels diminish. I should not have looked back.

As we moved upward, I get a sense of the temperature change. It is cool, but not cold. I inhaled the air. It is crisp and clean. I almost feel lightheaded. I held out my tongue to taste the air. I know that was silly; but I suspected that the air would taste sweet and pure, which it did.

We are now traveling through mist, but it is not moist. I look over to the "Man", but his expression has changed from watching me with ease to preparing for a strategic session with someone or something that appears to be as serious as life or death. This causes me to become alert.

As we approach our destination, I can see a city in the distance. The first thing I noticed is several domed buildings with gold roofs. The second is that the past influences some of the architecture. While, modern architecture has provided inspiration, too. There are detailed inscriptions and engraving on the buildings, gold inlaid streets and uniquely designed open spaces. The city is bright with a light that radiates from it. People, animals and other creatures that I have never seen before are coming and going in a peaceful and joyous manner. I paused above the city, trying to see everything and anything.

We traveled past the city to an open-air stadium or hall. Before I even realized it, I am sitting in my seat. Anticipation is in the air. Thousands of people are arriving at the same time. I am trying to take in all that I am seeing. I am astonished as to the differences between each individual. As I watch the comings and goings around me, I reflected on the last statement the "Man" made to me. He told me he was asked to bring me to Heaven, so I could witness the trial of man. I wonder to myself, "Why me?" and "Trial of Man?" I guess it is too late to clarify his statements. But clearly, I am in "Heaven" or a place within it.

I surveyed this huge and impressive arena. Okay, I have never seen anything like it. I cannot compare it to any place that I have ever been or experienced. It was not enclosed. There were no walls, no ceiling, or roof. It is the shape of a large circle with sections containing seats overlooking the center floor. It was completely open. It was above the clouds, but beneath the sun. The stars were in the distance. There were pillars that appeared to stretch as far as the eyes can see. The clouds give you the feeling of being in a light fog, yet it was crystal clear. Visibility was not an issue. As I looked down, I saw the earth with its land masses, mountains and the various bodies of waters. This was an unusual phenomenon. It appeared as if the earth was the floor of this arena.

The center of the arena was staged. It gives you an impression of a large courtroom. In the center, there was one large white throne with twelve smaller thrones to its right and twelve smaller thrones to its left, forming a semi-circle. People; not people. Ghosts; not ghost. There are no words that I can use that would adequately explain what I saw. Not Ghosts, but Spirits? Their appearance and form were like mist, transparent or translucent. You could tell that something or someone was there, but it is impossible to make out any of their personal or physical characteristics that would set one apart from the other. Their clothing, their crowns, their locations, and their aura would be what that differentiates one from the next.

The large white throne is beautiful. I have never seen anything like it. I don't believe anyone living has seen anything like I, either. Not unless they were here. There was a bright rainbow of many colors over the large white throne. It was decorated with various types of gemstones; gold with jasper, sapphire, agate, emerald, onyx, ruby, chrysolite, beryl, topaz, turquoise, jacinth, and amethyst. The person or persona on the large white throne was bright, radiating throughout the arena. Behind him appeared to be a fire. Not an enormous forest fire, but a fire the size of a campfire. It gave him a special glow. I bowed my head but raised my eyes so I can see him. I looked over to the Man and asked him, "***If that was God?***" and he said, ***"God is everywhere."*** I am in the presence of God . . . God! The entire arena feels like God. Just what you would expect; warm, safe and inviting.

After a period, I continued to take in the arena. Next to the large white throne were seven candlesticks with their holders that were also made of diamonds and gold. And behind the large white throne was a table. A meticulously carved wooden table with engravings of events from the past. Sitting upon the table was an engraved silver bowl with burning incense, which smelled throughout the arena.

There were four living creatures that surrounded the throne. Each creature had four heads, one of a man, an ox, an eagle, and a lion. They walked on all fours. Each of them had six wings. Two above their shoulders, two halfway down their back and two above their thighs. When they sat back on their hind legs, the wings would cover their bodies. These living creatures were covered with eyes. Eyes on their backs, their bodies and their wings. They had eyes all over them. And they walked around the large white throne, giving the appearance that they were on high alert, guarding the perimeter.

Each of the smaller thrones were bejeweled, however, they were not as spectacular as the large white one. The Spirits who sat on the smaller thrones were dressed in bright white, similar to "the Man," but the styles and designs varied. Yet, each of them wore a crown that was made of gold and jewels. From their thrones came lightning, thunder, rumbles, and vibrations. It caused the arena to have flashes of color, as well as the feeling of minor earthquakes.

At the podium, there was a Persona, a Spirit, who was dressed in purple and gold with shimmering flecks from the various gemstones that he wore. He, too, wore a crown. His was larger and with custom crafted designs; greater than those of the Spirits that sat on the twenty-four thrones, but not as glorious as the crown the Spirit on the Large White Throne wore. He came with an entourage. They sat in the area behind the podium, but in front of the twenty-four thrones. They, too, were decked out in colors and styles that were out of this world. While the Persona stood at the podium, there was a quality about him that could not be overlooked. He stood straight up and took in all that was before him. He appeared confident, determined, and ready. But despite his beauty and the beauty of his entourage, their presence was filled with darkness, altering the mood and the atmosphere.

There was tension in the arena and uncertainty in the air! It is he who is bringing the case against man. He is the "OPPOSITION, THE ADVERSARY." I am slowly putting the pieces of the puzzle together. There will be a trial of "man or humanity."

THANK YOU FOR YOUR SUPPORT

Please feel free to order the book, “Finding Peace” from Amazon, major retailers and bookstores near you.

Check out www.Brooksbooks.org or www.Brooksread.com

Made in the USA
Monee, IL
08 November 2021

81239086R10148